THE LIFE OF
MARTIN LUTHER KING, JR.

Leader for Civil Rights

Michael A. Schuman

 Enslow Publishers, Inc.
40 Industrial Road
Box 398
Berkeley Heights, NJ 07922
USA

http://www.enslow.com

To my editor, Damian Marie Palisi, who can push a writer
towards excellence with a velvet shove.

Originally published as *Martin Luther King, Jr.: Leader for Civil Rights* in 1996.

Library of Congress Cataloging-in-Publication Data

Schuman, Michael
    The life of Martin Luther King, Jr. : leader for civil rights / Michael A. Schuman.
      pages cm. — (Legendary African Americans)
    Includes bibliographical references and index. ISBN 978-0-7660-6147-7
    1. King, Martin Luther, Jr., 1929–1968 —Juvenile literature. 2. African Americans—
Biography—Juvenile literature. 3. Civil rights workers—United States—Biography—
Juvenile literature. 4. Baptists—United States—Clergy—Biography—Juvenile literature.
5. African Americans—Civil rights—History—20th century—Juvenile literature. I. Title.
E185.97.K5S386 2014
323.092—dc 3
[B]
                                2013050378

Future editions:
Paperback ISBN: 978-0-7660-6148-4
EPUB ISBN: 978-0-7660-6149-1
Single-User PDF ISBN: 978-0-7660-6150-7
Multi-User PDF ISBN: 978-0-7660-6151-4

Printed in the United States of America
072014 HF Group, North Manchester, IN
10 9 8 7 6 5 4 3 2 1

Illustration Credits: Library of Congress, p. 4.

Cover Illustration: Library of Congress

CONTENTS

Dr. Martin Luther King, Jr., was a powerful speaker, minister, and leader in the fight for civil rights. By using nonviolent means of protest and cooperation to advance the struggle for equality he became a national hero.

Chapter 1

A MOMENTOUS MOMENT IN WASHINGTON

D r. Martin Luther King, Jr., walked to a podium on a hot afternoon in Washington, D.C., in August 1963. Behind him was the Lincoln Memorial. King looked straight ahead and saw an ocean of humanity. The crowd was spread out like a fan before him. People surrounded a man-made body of water called the Reflecting Pool and stood tucked together in the shadows of a line of trees. In the distance was the Washington Monument, built in honor of the first President of the United States.

It is estimated that two hundred and fifty thousand men and women were there.[1] They were of all races and religions and came to support justice and equality for all Americans. They came by car, bus, train, airplane, bicycle, and foot.

The people had been listening for hours to speakers calling for equal rights and musicians performing songs of hope and good will. Dr. King was to be the last to speak. As he was introduced, hundreds of thousands of people chanted King's name. He was the person they most wanted to hear.

King gave the speech of his career, a speech that has since been accepted as one of the most important moments in American history.

The fact that King was at a landmark like the Lincoln Memorial to address this crowd was itself a remarkable achievement. He was only thirty-four years old, an age when many people are just gaining momentum in their careers. Ten years earlier he had been an unknown graduate student. Now he was the most famous and respected leader in the civil rights movement.

The movement had grown out of the frustration of African Americans living in the southern United States. In 1865 slavery was outlawed by the Thirteenth Amendment to the United States Constitution. Although African Americans were free from slavery, they were still not free from segregation.

Segregation, or separation of the races, was legal in the South. Public schools, restaurants, movie theaters, buses and trains, and even public bathrooms and drinking fountains were divided for "white" and "colored" use. (The term "African American" was unheard of then. Black persons were either called "colored" or what was at the time a more respectful term, "Negro.")

In addition, many elected and appointed officials in southern cities and towns took pleasure in brutalizing African Americans. Some belonged to a hate group called the Ku Klux Klan (KKK).

The huge rally that August day in Washington was officially called the March on Washington for Jobs and Freedom. It has since become known simply as the March on Washington. At the time, President John F. Kennedy had proposed a civil rights bill that would prohibit discrimination in hiring, voting, and access to public places. King and others thought an event like this would spur on passage of the bill.

King spoke words that day that have become part of history. He delivered them in slow, deliberate phrases and pronounced them carefully in a deep, baritone voice. King said that despite some gains, African Americans still suffered from bigotry and discrimination. Yet King always preached nonviolence and criticized those who said violence was an acceptable means of solving problems.

King said that day:

In the process of gaining our rightful place, we must not be guilty of wrongful deeds. Let us not seek to satisfy our thirst for freedom by drinking from the cup of bitterness and hatred. We must not allow our creative protest to degenerate into physical violence.[2]

The people cheered and applauded. Then he spoke words that have become legendary:

So, even though we face the difficulties of today and tomorrow, I still have a dream. It is a dream deeply rooted in the American dream. I have a dream that one day this nation will rise up and live out the true meaning of its creed: "We hold these truths to be self-evident—that all men are created equal." I have a dream that one day on the red hills of Georgia sons of former slaves and the sons of former slave owners will be able to sit down together at the table of brotherhood. . . . I have a dream that my four little children will one day live in a nation where they will not be judged by the color of their skin but by the content of their character.[3]

He concluded his speech with the words:

And when we allow freedom to ring . . . we will be able to speed up that day when all of God's children—black men and white men, Jews and Gentiles, Protestants and Catholics—will be able to join hands and to sing in the words of that old Negro spiritual, "Free at last! Free at last! Thank God Almighty, we are free at last."[4]

The crowd roared its approval.

The next year the Civil Rights Act of 1964 was passed.

Chapter 2

SEPARATE BUT UNEQUAL

Martin Luther King, Jr., was born in Atlanta, Georgia, at a time when the civil rights movement was a far-off vision. Legal segregation throughout the South was as common as magnolia blossoms in April. Yet the Atlanta neighborhood where Martin would grow up stood out as one of the most notable African-American communities in the nation.

King was born January 15, 1929, in a proud and handsome two-story home with a roomy front porch. It is located at 501 Auburn Avenue, east of downtown Atlanta. Because the neighborhood around Auburn Avenue was viewed as a center of opportunity for African Americans, it was known locally as "Sweet Auburn."

Around the time Martin was born, Sweet Auburn was home to African-American physicians, dentists, attorneys, and business leaders. In 1956 Auburn Avenue was called by the business magazine *Fortune* , "The Richest Negro Street in the World."

Yet Sweet Auburn was not without its poor. Mixed in with the two- and three-story Victorian homes were the shotgun row houses of the lower class. In many ways, it was like the United States in miniature with one exception. All of the residents were African American.

Although there were opportunities for African-American men in Martin's time and place, they were limited to this one neighborhood. For all the successes one saw in Sweet Auburn, one fact was plain. Atlanta, like the rest of the South, was segregated.

In addition, laws were passed that made it difficult for African Americans to vote. One law commonly enacted forced blacks to pass literacy tests for that right. No such tests were given to whites.

These laws were among many called Jim Crow laws. They were most likely named after a character in minstrel shows that toured from town to town in the 1800s. In these shows, white people would darken their faces with burnt cork and play the parts of blacks in a usually mocking manner. The role of Jim Crow and other characters made African Americans appear stupid and lazy.

The Jim Crow laws were based on the attitude that blacks were inferior to whites. The term commonly used for that belief is "white supremacy." White political leaders knew that with voting came power. They knew that if blacks were able to vote in numbers, white officeholders might lose their positions.

At the time, these racist laws were considered perfectly constitutional. A famous decision by the Supreme Court in 1896 confirmed that. The case was called *Plessy* v. *Ferguson*. The Supreme Court ruled in that case that the state of Louisiana was legally allowed to segregate railroad cars.

However, the overall effect of the case was much greater. It legalized the concept of "separate but equal" facilities for the races. In truth, facilities were separate but rarely equal. Schools, hotels, restaurants, and bathrooms for blacks were almost always dirty, run-down, or inferior in other ways to those for whites. Considering all the limitations for African Americans, it is amazing that Sweet Auburn was able to thrive as it did.

This was the world into which Martin Luther King, Jr., was born. His given name at birth was Michael King, son of Michael Luther King. But his name was changed to Martin Luther King, Jr., when he was five.

Why his name was changed is not clear. Dean Rowley, historian at Martin Luther King National Historic Site in Atlanta, said there are two separate stories. According to one, Martin's father changed his son's name out of respect for his late father (Martin's grandfather), who had always preferred the name Martin Luther. Another version says that Martin's father had attended an international Baptist convention in Germany in the early 1930s and was impressed by European Protestantism. He changed his son's name to reflect his newfound respect for the sixteenth-century Protestant religious reformer, Martin Luther.

Dean Rowley explained that because there were no formal requirements to register name changes when Martin was a boy, there are no records and the truth is a mystery.

At any rate, the youngster was known not by either name as a child but by his initials, M.L.

When M.L. was born, his father was assistant pastor and his grandfather was pastor at Ebenezer Baptist Church, one of the most respected churches in Atlanta's African-American community. Two years later, M.L.'s grandfather died as a result of a stroke, and his father became pastor. The church was located just down the road from the King home. M.L. would spend nearly as much time there as in his home.

M.L. had two siblings. His sister, Willie Christine, was a year older. She was known as Chris. His brother, Alfred Daniel, was a year younger and was called A.D. The children called their parents Daddy and Mother Dear.

The King household was a loving one. Still, Daddy King believed strongly in discipline and would hit the hand or spank the backside of his children with a stick or belt if they misbehaved. At the time, such discipline was not unusual in families or even in schools.

Playtime at home did not begin until chores were completed. One chore was washing dishes. It was a job the children rotated and one that M.L. protested because he believed dish washing was women's work.

M.L. and his siblings also objected when it came time to learn piano. Their mother taught piano to neighborhood children and tried to teach her own. They did not take well to the lessons and would pound on the piano in the parlor, hoping that if they damaged it their lessons would cease.

M.L. did enjoy singing. He could often be found belting out gospel songs in church while his mother played piano. His favorite song was "I Want to Be Like Jesus." M.L.'s singing was so well liked that he was sometimes hired to perform at religious revival meetings and conventions.

Fun time indoors consisted of board games such as Monopoly and card games such as Old Maid. Outdoors M.L. liked riding his bicycle and playing team sports. He was known for being tough. During one baseball game, M.L. was catching and A.D. was at bat. A.D. swung at a pitch and missed. His bat fell loose and whacked M.L. on the head, knocking him to the ground. M.L. got up right away and said, "All right, A.D., you're out."[1]

The King children also played with other young people in the neighborhood. In the years before M.L. was old enough to go to school, his best friends were two white boys whose father owned a grocery store across the street from M.L.'s home. (The Kings lived just a few blocks from a white section of Atlanta, where the grocer and his family lived.)

When the boys reached age six, in 1935, they were sent to separate public schools. M.L. was sent to a school that was all black. His friends went to a school that was all white.

King recalled:

They went to the white school and I went to another, and I still didn't think much about it at first. But suddenly when I would run across the street after school to compare notes, their mother would tell them that they could not play (with me) anymore. She said they were white and I was colored. . . . I think I cried, but anyway I rushed home and asked mother about it.[2]

M.L.'s mother told him the painful truth. She described how their ancestors were taken against their will from Africa to be used as slaves and how the Civil War freed the slaves. She further explained how African Americans were supposed to be free but were still under control of laws that were not fair. She said prejudice came from fear.

She knew M.L. was heartbroken about not being able to play with his white friends. So she said, "Don't let this thing impress you. Don't let it make you feel you are not as good as white people. You are as good as anyone else, and don't you forget it."[3]

But he was not allowed to forget racism either. Two years later M.L. and his father went into downtown Atlanta to buy a pair of shoes. A white clerk told them he would serve them if they moved to the rear of their store. Daddy King would not do that, and he took M.L. and angrily left.

King recalled his father saying, "I don't care how long I have to live with this system, I am never going to accept it. I'll oppose it until the day I die."[4]

M.L. was emotional like his father. Like many boys, M.L. and his brother enjoyed roughhousing. One time A.D. slid down a bannister and accidently knocked down their grandmother. She was motionless. The two young brothers thought they had killed her.

According to several biographies, M.L. responded by climbing to the second floor of the house and jumping out of the window. His family screamed his name, but M.L. remained motionless. When he heard that his grandmother was all right, he simply got up and walked away.

When M.L. was twelve, his grandmother died. In shock, it is said that he again jumped from the second -story window. Just as before, his family called to him. Finally, M.L. got up.

Whether King was trying to commit suicide or reacted in this manner for another reason is not known. But these were actions of a sensitive and emotional youngster.

It is interesting to note that King's sister, Christine King Farris, has a different version of those events. According to Dean Rowley at the Martin Luther King National Historic Site:

> Christine says that Martin liked to show off when he was a little boy, and whenever he wanted to show off, he would put on a cape or choir robe to look like Superman and jump out the second-story window. Christine says the two incidents (described above) never happened.[5]

However emotional he was, M.L. was also a very good student. He did well in math and enjoyed history and English. He was a poor speller but practiced hard on vocabulary, using language that impressed both his teachers and fellow students. He did so well in school that he skipped ninth grade and entered Booker T. Washington High School at age thirteen in 1942.

M.L. also had a rebellious streak. He was respectful of his teachers, but he found ways to lash out against authority. The closest authority figure was Daddy. M.L. knew he wanted some day to serve mankind, but he wanted to be different from his father. So he decided he would not be a preacher.

M.L. questioned the fundamentalist teachings in Daddy's church. King remembered that at age thirteen, "I shocked my Sunday School class by denying the bodily resurrection of Jesus."[6]

In high school, M.L. also discovered girls. He had a deep, resonant voice that girls found attractive, and he was a sharp dresser. Friends called him "Tweed" because he liked to wear tweed sport coats. He dated girls from some of the most respected African-American families in Atlanta. King later admitted that his two biggest weaknesses were food and women.

His brother A.D. remembered, "He kept flitting from chick to chick, and I decided I couldn't keep up with him. Especially since he was crazy about dances, and just about the best jitterbug in town."[7]

When King was in high school, World War II (1939–1945) was raging. Because so many young men were fighting in the war, there was a shortage of college students. In Atlanta, all-black, all-male Morehouse College decided to admit high school juniors with excellent records. M.L.'s father was a Morehouse graduate, and M.L. took and passed the college entrance examinations in the spring of 1944. He graduated high school as a junior and chose to attend Morehouse as a freshman in the fall. He was fifteen years old.

Just before he graduated, King entered a speaking contest in southern Georgia. His topic was "The Negro and the Constitution," and King won an award for his talk. But what should have been one of the most exciting nights of his life became a shameful one.

On the ride back to Atlanta, the bus driver told King and the other African-American students to move to the rear of the bus. They refused. The driver yelled at the students, calling them, "black sons of bitches."[8] The teacher with the students quietly suggested it would be best if they did as the bus driver said. So they did.

Years later King said, "It was a night I'll never forget. I don't think I have ever been so deeply angry in my life."[9]

That summer King and other Morehouse students took jobs picking cigar tobacco outside Hartford, Connecticut, in the small town of Simsbury. It was hard work in the muggy Connecticut River Valley. But King enjoyed a personal freedom he had never experienced before.

On weekends King and his coworkers went to Hartford for fun and relaxation. There they could eat alongside white people at the same restaurants and sit alongside whites in the same theaters. The contrast between Hartford and Atlanta was startling.

So was the train ride back to Atlanta. While the train rolled through Connecticut, New York, New Jersey, and Maryland, King was able to eat in the main dining car with white riders. Once the train reached Virginia, he had to move to a rear table. A curtain blocked King from the white diners' view.

King sat in the train staring at the curtain. He wondered why other people would find a view of him to be offensive. He said, "I felt as though the curtain had dropped on my selfhood."[10]

Chapter 3

THE COLLEGIATE CLERIC

K ing entered his freshman year of college in the fall of 1944. He was a short, pudgy-faced teenager several years younger than most of his classmates.

Most students lived on campus, but because of his age, King lived at home. He commuted to classes by trolley. The girls he dated were in high school, not college. He was detached from campus activities.

King also was undecided about a career path. Some college students choose a career as a means of making money in a field they find fun. King wanted a profession that would permit him to help African Americans. He considered becoming a doctor, then a lawyer. He finally settled on a major in sociology and a minor in English.

Despite his youth and indecision, King was recognized as a bright young scholar by his teachers. The president of Morehouse College at the time was a tall, gray-haired minister named Dr. Benjamin Mays. In his later years, Mays said about King, "He had a balance and maturity then that were far beyond his years and a grasp of life and its problems which exceeded even that."[1]

Mays had a huge influence over King. He spoke at weekly campus chapel services that King attended regularly. M.L. enjoyed talking with Mays afterward about his sermons.

Mays was also a member of the National Association for the Advancement of Colored People (NAACP). The NAACP is an organization formed in 1909 to fight discrimination against minorities, especially African Americans.

In the 1940s, it was dangerous for any black person in the South to be a known member of the NAACP or to speak out publicly against the system of Jim Crow laws. Outspoken African Americans and their supporters received threats from racists. The Ku Klux Klan was notorious for this.

Much of the time these bigots acted on their threats. African-American-owned homes and churches were bombed. African Americans were commonly lynched. Lynching is executing a person not convicted of a crime. The usual form of lynching was hanging.

Benjamin Mays did speak out against segregation, and this impressed King. Mays told Morehouse students that education was the key to freedom for African Americans.

King's other big influence at Morehouse was a religion professor named George D. Kelsey. Before meeting Kelsey, King had doubts about religion.[2] King had been raised as a fundamentalist. Fundamentalists believe every word in the Bible is to be taken literally. But facts King learned in history classes contradicted stories in the Bible.

Kelsey helped solve King's dilemma. The professor told King "to see that behind the legends and myths of the Book were many profound truths which one could not escape."[3]

King later said that thanks to Kelsey, "the shackles of fundamentalism were removed from my body."[4]

In addition, both Mays and Kelsey stressed that modern ministers should address social ills in addition to religion. This set a fire under King. Although he had wanted to separate himself from his father's influence, he began to feel comfortable with the idea of entering the ministry.

Like many college students, King spent his summers working to earn expense money. As the son of a well-known man in Atlanta's African-American community, he could have easily gotten a comfortable job working for an African-American-owned business. But he wanted to see what life was like for poor people. So he took jobs as a manual laborer.

At one job, he unloaded trucks and trains in the sweltering summer heat. At another, he worked in a stockroom and on a loading platform. Daddy King was against his son taking these jobs. He thought white supervisors would insult and abuse his son.

As it turned out, Daddy King was right. White supervisors called King names like "nigger." King also noticed that black workers were paid less than white workers for the same jobs. Still, Martin received from these jobs what he wanted—an education about how poor people lived and worked.

As King grew older, college activities started to play a larger part in his life. He made the football team and sang in the glee club. He also spent less time with high school girls. He preferred the company of students from Spelman College, a women's college associated with Morehouse.

King was also part of an organization in Atlanta called the Intercollegiate Council. The council was an integrated group of students from various Atlanta colleges. King's membership in this group played a very important role in his attitudes towards race.

Before he joined the council, most of his relations with white people had been hostile. But the white students in the Intercollegiate Council treated him as an equal. And they were sympathetic to the plight of African Americans.

King later said, "I had been ready to resent the whole white race, but as I got to see more white people my resentment was softened and a spirit of cooperation took its place."[5]

In his junior year at Morehouse, Martin told his father he wanted to be a minister. Daddy King arranged for his son to deliver a trial sermon in a small room in his church. Martin's sermon so intrigued the people that the small hall was soon filled to capacity. King had to move to the main auditorium to finish.

His father was so pleased that night that he got on his knees and thanked God for his son.[6] Martin was ordained a minister in 1947 and at the same time was named assistant pastor of the church.

King graduated from Morehouse in the spring of 1948 with a bachelor of arts degree in sociology. He was nineteen years old. His next goal was to earn a bachelor's degree in divinity in a northern city where there was no segregation. King's first choice was Crozer Theological Seminary in Chester, Pennsylvania, outside Philadelphia. He got his wish and was accepted at Crozer.

By this time, he had traded his initials for his given name. Dean Rowley says, "Like many young men, he was trying to differentiate himself from his father. By the time he went to grad school at Crozer, he was referring to himself as Martin."[7]

The campus was located in a cozy, wooded setting high on a hill overlooking Chester. It was also overwhelmingly white. Of the approximately one hundred students enrolled in Crozer, only six were African-American.

At first King was self-conscious about his race.[8] At the time, many white people prejudged blacks as being lazy, loud, and late. Some still do. King was aware of this and tried to be prompt, well-dressed, and serious.

His courses included church history, views of the prophets, Biblical criticism, and social philosophy. He also examined the works of many philosophers. One who influenced him the most was a man named Walter Rauschenbusch, a minister who taught in the 1890s and early 1900s in Rochester, New York. Rauschenbusch believed that Christianity would do the most good if used to promote brotherhood among people. He believed Christianity should be a tool for improving people's economic and social conditions.

Rauschenbusch wrote:

It is the function of religion to teach the individual to value his soul more than his body, and his moral integrity more than his income. In the same way it is the function of religion to teach society to value human life more than property, and to value property only in so far as it forms the material basis for the higher development of human life.[9]

Rauschenbusch also strongly criticized capitalism, which is the economic system of the United States. In capitalism, services and goods are produced by private businesses. Those who believe in capitalism say people will be better workers and produce more when rewarded with personal incentives like better wages or bonuses. Rauschenbusch's view was that the basis of capitalism was greed. He said that capitalism was responsible for poverty.

Another philosopher King studied was Karl Marx, who lived in Germany in the 1800s. Marx was a proponent of a form of pure communism now known as Marxism. In Marxism all business is owned by the government. Those who believe in Marxism believe people will produce best when working for the community as a whole and do not need special incentives.

King agreed with Marx that there was much economic unfairness in the world. But he strongly believed that communism was not an answer to such problems. He thought communism stripped people of their individuality. More importantly, King was disturbed by the communist belief that there was no God.

One Sunday King attended a lecture given by the president of Howard University, a predominantly black college in Washington, D.C. The man's name was Dr. Mordecai W. Johnson, and he had just returned from fifty days in India.

At that time, India was being ruled by Great Britain. The people of India wanted to live under their own rule rather than that of a faraway country. In addition, Great Britain was mainly a Christian, Anglo-Saxon nation while the people of India were mostly Hindus and Muslims.

The struggle in India was led by a man named Mohandas K. Gandhi. He had earned the title Mahatma, given to Hindu people regarded for high moral and spiritual character. Many simply referred to him as Mahatma Gandhi.

Gandhi's philosophy in leading the movement was civil disobedience. Gandhi himself had learned about this idea from the writings of an American named Henry David Thoreau, who lived in the 1800s.

Civil disobedience means protesting peacefully against unjust laws. One was never to resort to violence. At times, this meant being hit or beaten without fighting back. Gandhi believed that hatred and violence only bred more hatred and violence. He believed peaceful protest would avoid bitter feelings between both sides when the conflict was over.

He believed civil disobedience was effective for two main reasons. For one, neutral observers would feel compassion for unarmed and nonviolent victims. In addition, when convicted of violating unjust laws, masses of protestors would be sent to jail. If the jails were overflowing with nonviolent protestors, it would prove that the laws were not working. As a result, they would be changed.

Fighting against the British government, Gandhi put Thoreau's ideas to use in the form of protest marches, strikes, boycotts, and fasts. King was impressed with Johnson's talk and Gandhi's techniques.

King soon had a chance to put Gandhi's basic philosophy into action. At most colleges, students play pranks on one another for laughs with no ill intent. This was true even at the seminary. One such antic was a "room raid," in which a student's room was purposely messed up or rearranged.

One time the target was a white student from North Carolina named Lucius Z. Hall, Jr. Hall was known for his bigotry and did not find the "room raid" funny. He blamed King and ran into his room, waving a gun.[10]

In response, King remained calm. He told Hall he had nothing to do with the raid. King refused to fight back, threaten, or shout.

Other students in the dormitory persuaded Hall to put down his gun. He did.

The incident was brought up before the student government, but King did not press charges. His grace and maturity impressed the students. Hall eventually apologized. By the time King graduated, he and Hall had become friends.

King graduated Crozer with a Bachelor of Divinity degree in June 1951. He maintained an A average for all three years and was named valedictorian of his class. The valedictorian is the student who graduates with the best grades. King also won an award as the most outstanding student in his class and was given a $1,300 scholarship to the graduate school of his choice.

Chapter 4

MARRIAGE AND
A MAJOR MOVE

King's choice of graduate school was Boston University in Massachusetts, home to a well-respected school of theology. Theology is the study of religion and the nature of God.

One reason for King's decision was a professor named Dr. Edgar Sheffield Brightman. This professor was known and admired for his writings on religion. King had read and studied Brightman's works since he was a student at Morehouse.

King spent the summer after his graduation from Crozer preaching at Ebenezer Baptist Church. His father promoted him to associate pastor, which gave him even more responsibility. At times, King, Sr., would leave town so Martin could run a service by himself.

When summer had turned into fall, King loaded his belongings into a green Chevrolet his parents gave him as a graduation present. The young man again drove north and in September 1951, he began his studies toward a doctorate of philosophy (Ph.D.).

At first King lived a distance from campus. During his second semester, he teamed up with an old friend from Morehouse named Philip Lenud, and the two rented a suite closer to campus. Lenud was a graduate student studying in a similar program. However, Lenud was enrolled at Tufts University in the city of Medford, just outside Boston.

Lenud was a good cook and prepared most of the two men's meals. King did his part by cleaning the dishes. Unlike when he was a child, Martin did not complain about the job this time.

Lenud and King often had discussions about philosophy. In time they invited other African-American male friends in Boston to join them on a Friday or Saturday evening. One would usually read out loud a paper on some philosophical belief, and the men would spend the evening discussing it. They called their little group the Philosophical Club.

Word of this exchange of ideas spread among other students. Before long, women and white students joined. Those in the group enjoyed exchanging their thoughts and ideas as they sat together, drinking hot coffee on chilly Boston evenings.

Soon there was a tragedy that affected King's studies. His idol, Dr. Brightman, died when King was in his second year at Boston University. King was terribly saddened and often cried when he thought of his teacher.[1]

King's new advisor was Professor L. Harold DeWolf. King became as impressed with DeWolf as he had been with Brightman. Both Brightman and DeWolf helped shape two beliefs King would have all his life. One was that the true God was a personal one. The other was that every human being is one of dignity and worth. This meant to King that people were basically good. They could cast out evil if only they accepted God's basic love and goodness.

But King's life as a student was not all seriousness. Away from his studies, he had an active social life. He and Lenud went out together often. They liked going to night clubs and restaurants that served soul food. King also dated frequently and was known among single women in the college community as a great catch.

Still, he was not in love with any of the women he dated. One January day in 1952 he was eating lunch with a married friend named Mary Powell in a soul food restaurant called the Western Lunch Box. Powell was from Atlanta, and King had met her when he was at Morehouse and she was a student at Spelman.

Over lunch, King said to Powell, "Mary, I wish I knew a few girls from down home to go out with. I tell you, these Boston girls are something else. The ones I've been seeing are so reserved."[2]

Powell mentioned two names. One was a woman King already knew. The other was a woman named Coretta Scott. Coretta was from Alabama and a student at the New England Conservatory of Music. She was studying voice and hoping to become a classical singer. Powell described this young woman as intelligent, pretty, and personable.

Powell then told Coretta about the young Baptist minister who was studying for his Ph.D. When Coretta heard the man was a minister, she lost interest. She imagined ministers to be stuffy and prim.[3]

Martin called Coretta on the phone and began to charm her with words. She remembered:

I had never heard such talk in all my life. He said, "You know every Napoleon has his Waterloo. I'm like Napoleon. I'm at my Waterloo, and I'm on my knees."

I must admit I enjoyed the fun. We had a long conversation in which he asked me about my studies and told me a little about his work under Professor Edgar S. Brightman.

Finally he said, "I'd like to meet you and talk some more. Perhaps we could have lunch tomorrow or something like that."[4]

The two made a date for lunch the next day. Coretta waited for Martin on the steps outside the conservatory in the cold winter drizzle. When she saw the green Chevrolet pull up, she walked down the steps and approached the car.

She later wrote that her first thoughts were, "How short he seems" and "How unimpressive he looks."[5]

But those thoughts did not last. King complimented Scott on her long hair. In response, Scott was a bit flustered, but she tried to remain poised.

Scott later said:

It was a little difficult, for in those few minutes I had forgotten about Martin being short and had completely revised my first impression. He radiated charm. When he talked, he grew in stature. Even when he was so young, he drew people to him from the very first moment with his eloquence, his sincerity, and his moral stature. I knew immediately that he was very special.[6]

Martin and Coretta's second date was a party. On the way to the party, the couple stopped to see Mary Powell. Martin told her, "Mary, I owe you a thousand dollars for introducing me to this girl."[7]

Coretta reacted coolly, but was impressed.[8]

As Martin and Coretta continued dating, they became closer. Dates included concerts at Symphony Hall, walks along the beach in the summer, and ice skating in the winter. The two often talked about philosophy and found they had similar ideas on race and attitudes.

From the first date, Martin discussed the idea of marriage to Coretta. She was a little put off by that, since she planned to carve out her own career as a singer. In the 1950s, it was often expected that when a couple married, the man would keep his career and the woman would often give up hers. It was a woman's accepted role to be a wife and mother.

Coretta considered the matter and decided she would put her career on hold and marry Martin. The wedding took place on the front lawn of her parents' home in Alabama on June 18, 1953. Daddy King performed the ceremony.

The newlyweds moved back to Boston in the fall of 1953. They rented a four-room apartment and put their energies into finishing their studies. By the end of the school year in 1954, Coretta received her degree, and Martin was studying job offers from both churches and universities.

King was not sure if he wanted to preach in a church or teach in a college setting. His idol, Benjamin Mays, was a minister who taught. But Mays was a pastor in a church for many years before he became a professor. King decided to follow Mays' career path.

The next step was selecting a church. King received offers from two churches in the North. Meanwhile, churches in Chattanooga, Tennessee, and Montgomery, Alabama, also expressed interest in him. Coretta leaned toward a northern church. She had had enough of the legal segregation that existed in the South.

But Martin felt that in spite of all the problems, the South was his home. He had an urge to reach the African Americans who lived there. He decided that the South was where he could do the most good.

On April 14, 1954, King accepted a position at the Dexter Avenue Baptist Church in Montgomery. It was just two hours away from both his and Coretta's parents' homes. Also, many members of the church were professionals and teachers from nearby Alabama State College. They were a bit more intellectual than the members of the church in Chattanooga. And they were less apt to be fundamentalist. This was attractive to King. The Kings made plans to leave Boston and move to Montgomery.

Just a month after King accepted the job in Montgomery, there was a major decision handed down by the United States Supreme Court. It was called *Brown* v. *Board of Education of Topeka, Kansas.* The court ruled that the concept of "separate but equal" was unconstitutional as it related to public schools. Suddenly, the entire system of school segregation was illegal.

This sent shock waves throughout the South. In anger, southern whites randomly attacked blacks. Those favoring segregation, which included most southern government leaders, vowed not to comply with the court's ruling. In Alabama, the State Board of Education voted unanimously to keep their school segregated, regardless of what the Supreme Court had decided. The whole southern system of white supremacy was in chaos.

This was the world Martin and Coretta Scott King entered when they moved to Montgomery in 1954.

Chapter 5

MONTGOMERY

The Kings settled into a routine as soon as they moved into their home. There were few spare moments in Martin's day.

He had some work to do to complete his Ph.D. That meant waking up around 5:30 A.M. to work on it for a few hours. The rest of the day was spent on church business. King also became involved with the local chapter of the NAACP and attended their meetings.

Finally King earned his Ph.D. in June 1955. He was officially Doctor Martin Luther King, Jr.

Now that he no longer had to spend hours on studies, King became more active in the NAACP. He was appointed to the local chapter's executive committee.

Coretta filled the traditional role of wife and, soon, mother. On November 17, 1955, she gave birth to a daughter named Yolanda Denise, called "Yoki" as a nickname.

In the South, African Americans were beginning to stand up for their rights more often. The *Brown* decision had given them some political clout, and the NAACP legally challenged a few cases of continued segregation.

Overall, however, segregation was still widespread throughout the South. The idea of mixing with blacks caused many whites to become angry. Whites were used to being treated as superiors. They raised their children to feel superior to blacks. Some white ministers would take verses out of context from the Bible to "prove" that white supremacy was the will of God. They would twist around the verse's meaning to support their views. One favorite verse was from Paul from the New Testament: "Servant, be obedient to your master."[1]

Now their superiority was being challenged. Tensions ran high.

In spite of the *Brown* decision, many African Americans, especially older ones set in their ways, were scared to stand up for their rights. They knew there was always a chance they could be beaten or killed for doing so. They also knew that juries in the South rarely convicted whites of murdering blacks.

In Montgomery, city buses were segregated. If blacks rode the same buses as whites, they had to sit in the back. If every seat was occupied and a white person entered, a black person had to give his or her seat to the white man or woman. At times an elderly black man or woman might stand for an entire ride while a young white person sat.

Even if seats in the white section were empty, it was illegal for blacks to occupy them. Blacks could not even occupy a seat parallel to that of a white.

An African-American high school student named Claudette Colvin was arrested in March 1955 for sitting parallel to a white person and refusing to give up her seat. She later remembered:

The police knocked my books down. One took one wrist, the other grabbed the other, and they were pulling me off the bus, just like you see on the TV now. . . . Someone must have said they didn't have handcuffs on me, and I might run away, so they put handcuffs on me. And then they took me to City Hall. I remember one of the men saying, "What happened to this black bitch? This is a black whore." He said, "Take her to Atmore (the state prison) and get rid of her."[2]

King served on a committee of local African Americans to protest the arrest. Representatives of the bus company and the police met with the committee. They were polite and promised action would be taken. But nothing was done.

After the Colvin incident, the local NAACP started looking for another case to test the bus segregation law. It happened on a dark and cold December evening in 1955.

Most residents of Montgomery were on their way home after a day's work. Few paid attention to Rosa Parks, a small black woman who boarded the Cleveland Avenue bus. None could have imagined that she was about to make history.

Parks was a seamstress at a department store. Every day she rode this same bus to and from work. Like most workers heading home, Parks just wanted a place to sit and rest. She occupied an empty seat next to a black man in the first row of the black section. At two further stops, white people boarded the bus and legally took the seats of other black passengers, forcing them to stand.

At the third stop, still more white passengers entered and found seats. However, one white man was left standing. The bus driver, J. P. Blake, turned and told Parks, the man sitting next to her, and two women in the seat across from her they must forfeit their seats. But none did.

Then Blake called out, "You better make it light on yourselves and let me have those seats."[3]

Fearful of getting arrested, the man next to Parks and the two women across from her all stood and moved to the rear. But Parks merely slid over to the window side of her seat.

"Look, woman," ordered Blake, "I told you I wanted that seat. Are you going to stand up?"

Parks simply replied, "No."

Blake responded, "If you don't stand up, I'm going to have you arrested."[4]

Parks told him to go ahead and do so. She was not going to move.

The driver left the bus in a huff and called the police. Parks remained seated. Meanwhile, several other passengers left the bus to find other means of transportation.

The driver returned, and within a few minutes, two police officers arrived. The driver pointed to Parks. One officer asked why she refused to stand when ordered to do so.

Parks replied, "I don't think I should have to. Why do you push us around so?"

The police officer answered, "I don't know, but the law is the law, and you are under arrest."[5]

The police escorted Parks off the bus. She was taken to police headquarters, then the city jail. She was later found guilty and fined $14 for breaking the city's segregation law.

Rosa Parks's refusal to get out of her seat has since become a legendary event in the history of civil rights movement. Over the years, it has been said that Parks did not stand because she was tired and her feet were sore. But forty years later, Parks said that was not the case.

"The real story is that I did not want to be treated in this manner. . . . I didn't feel it was helping me as an individual or us as a people for me to stand up just because he (Blake) said, 'Get up off the seat.'"[6]

This was the test case the NAACP had been looking for. They knew Parks's character and background would be examined closely by the police and the media. Parks was an intelligent, upstanding, hard-working woman. She had served as a secretary for the Montgomery NAACP and was liked and respected in the local African-American community. It would be hard for city leaders or white supremacists to taint her reputation.

Word spread in the community that an African American had been arrested for violating the bus segregation law. A local leader of the NAACP named E. D. Nixon was contacted. Nixon called King at his church and excitedly told him that they had their test case.

Nixon suggested to King that African Americans no longer ride the city buses until the segregation law was abolished. This type of peaceful resistance is called a boycott.

King agreed and contacted another Montgomery minister named Ralph David Abernathy. King and Abernathy had become friends since King moved to the city. Abernathy also agreed that a boycott was in order. A conference of African-American leaders was held that night at King's church. It was decided the boycott would begin the coming Monday, December 5.

King and others distributed thousands of leaflets over the weekend. The leaflets read:

Another Negro has been arrested and put in jail because she refused to give up her bus seat. Don't ride the buses to work, to town, to school, or anywhere on Monday, December 5. If you work, take a cab, or share a ride, or walk. Come to a mass meeting Monday night at 7 o'clock at the Holt Street Baptist Church.[7]

In churches on Sunday, African-American ministers told their congregations about the plan. Nixon also told the biggest daily newspaper in Montgomery, the white-owned *Montgomery Advertiser*, about the boycott. The paper ran a huge article in the large Sunday edition. The newspaper staff was getting a scoop. But by running the article, they also alerted African Americans who had not seen the leaflet or gone to church.

In addition, the Montgomery police commissioner, Clyde Summers, went on local television that weekend to condemn the upcoming boycott. Summers claimed African-American thugs were going to stop other African Americans from riding the buses. Although he did not realize it, Summers was also giving free publicity about the boycott.

To be successful, the boycott effort needed mass cooperation. In spite of the publicity, King still had doubts that it would work.[8]

Monday morning, December 5, dawned. Martin and Coretta King were up and dressed by 5:30 A.M., earlier than they usually rose. They ate breakfast, then Coretta walked into their living room and looked out the window. The 6:00 A.M. bus rolled by. Coretta shouted, "Martin! Martin!, come quickly!"

She later wrote, "He ran in and stood beside me, his face lit with excitement. There was not one person on that usually crowded bus!"[9]

The situation was the same throughout the city. The boycott was working. Montgomery's African-American citizens felt enough was enough. They either drove or got rides to work. Some walked rather than ride the buses.

African-American leaders knew the boycott would have to last more than one day to be effective. They immediately formed a group to decide future plans of action. It was called the Montgomery Improvement Association (MIA).

The MIA needed a president. King was only twenty-six years old, and one local minister said he looked "more like a boy than a man."[10] Yet he was intelligent and articulate, and the MIA members thought he would be a superb spokesperson. King was chosen, and a momentous career as an activist had begun.

From the start, city officials did everything they could to end the boycott without abolishing the segregation law. King and the rest of the MIA were seen as "Negro" radicals who must be stopped. But the boycott continued into the new year. On January 21, 1956, city leaders announced to the press that a compromise settlement had been reached. The announcement was printed in the local newspaper.

But there was no such settlement. City officials had lured three African-American ministers, unaffiliated with the MIA, into a meeting. After the meeting, the officials and the three ministers announced a settlement to the press. This "settlement" continued segregated seating but called for bus drivers to be more courteous to African Americans.

Leaders of the MIA told ministers to tell their parishioners that the settlement was phony and the boycott was still on. And it continued.

Montgomery city officials then decided to try to put an end to the boycott by harassing African-American motorists. Many were using their own cars to drive others to jobs. Police stopped cars driven by African Americans and gave them tickets for trivial or completely false traffic violations.

King himself was stopped on January 26 for exceeding the speed limit. In truth, he was driving well under the limit.[11] King was taken away and locked in jail until bail could be arranged. Because of the late hour that was not possible. Meanwhile, African Americans began gathering outside the jail in protest. This concerned the white officers inside, and they released King on his own recognizance. This was his first time ever in a jail cell. It would not be his last.

There were threats to King's safety. He received hate letters and harassing phone calls. On January 27, the phone rang in the middle of the night. The voice said, "Listen, nigger. We've taken all we want from you. Before next week you'll be sorry you ever came to Montgomery."[12]

Three nights later King was at Abernathy's church when he got word that his home had been bombed. He rushed home to find Coretta and baby Yoki scared but unharmed.

An angry crowd of several hundred African Americans had gathered in front of his house. Tempers were flaring. Some black men threatened white police officers with guns. Others were armed with broken bottles. They blamed the police and the white authorities in Montgomery for creating the climate that caused the bombing. Insults and threats flew.

Then King stepped onto his front porch and addressed the crowd. He said:

If you have weapons, take them home; if you do not have them, please do not seek to get them. We cannot solve this problem through retaliatory violence. We must meet violence with nonviolence. . . . If I am stopped, our work will not stop, for what we are doing is right. What we are doing is just—and God is with us.[13]

Andrew Young, a longtime associate of King, recalled that night. He said King "made a very eloquent statement that if we follow the teaching of an eye for an eye and a tooth for a tooth, we'll end up with a nation of people who are blind and toothless."[14]

The crowd broke up and went to their homes.

Two days later E. D. Nixon's home was bombed. Again, there were no injuries.

As the boycott continued, King became very concerned about his safety. At one point, he went to local police headquarters and applied for a gun permit. When asked why, King replied, "For self-defense."[15]

The police asked him, "Against whom?" Even though there were constant threats against his life, King could not name any one person, and his request was denied.[16]

Word soon spread around the city that this man who preached nonviolence was trying to buy a gun. It was an embarrassment for King, who was ashamed of what he tried to do. Nationally-known black leaders, when asked about the incident, had nothing to say.[17]

Meanwhile, Daddy King was urging his son to come back home to Atlanta where he would be safe. These requests from his father continued as the boycott stretched into spring. Daddy King had heard that the city's next step was to arrest the MIA leaders under an obscure state antiboycotting law. But Martin said he would stay in Montgomery. He said the people there were counting on him.

About ninety MIA leaders, including King, were arrested and found guilty of violating the antiboycott law. They were sentenced to pay fines. But the boycott continued.

News of the mass arrests and convictions made newspapers all over the country. Again, a city action had backfired. The boycott was gaining sympathy across the country.

It went on through the summer. Special car pools took African Americans to and from work in station wagons. Some who walked to work were beaten by angry whites or hit with bricks and garbage. In August, another home was bombed. It belonged to Reverend Robert Graetz, a white minister of a black Lutheran church and the only white member of the MIA.

The boycott continued into the fall. In September the auto insurance policies on many of the MIA's station wagons were cancelled. Private cars had to be used for weeks until the MIA obtained new insurance coverage.

In late October, the city thought of another action it hoped would stop the boycott. It claimed the bus company had an exclusive right to provide all mass transit in Montgomery. It said the MIA's car pool was a form of mass transit and violated that right. King and other MIA leaders went to court on Tuesday, November 13, as this case was to be heard.

In the late morning that day, a reporter approached King with some welcome news. The United States Supreme Court ruled that bus segregation in Montgomery was illegal. The ruling would take effect as soon as the court order was formally delivered in Montgomery in a few days.

On the same day, a judge in Montgomery declared the MIA's car pool was illegal. It did not matter since the Supreme Court decision overruled the Montgomery decision.

But there was one more delay. The city of Montgomery was able to appeal the decision. That means it was permitted to ask the Supreme Court to reconsider its decision, which it did. Since the car pool was now legally banned, African Americans had to scramble around for rides to work while the decision was being reconsidered.

Finally, on Monday, December 17, the Supreme Court rejected the city's last attempt to stop the order. United States marshals served the order in Montgomery around noon on December 20. After more than a year, the boycott was over. Bus segregation was ended. And the next day, Martin Luther King, Jr., and a white friend sat side by side in the front of a city bus and went for a ride through Montgomery.

Chapter 6

SPIRITUAL
STRATEGY

Two days after the historic bus ride, an unknown person fired a shotgun at King's house. The family was asleep, and no one was hurt. Over the next few days, buses were shot at, and one person was injured. On January 10, 1957, the homes of Robert Graetz and Ralph Abernathy were bombed, along with several African-American churches.

On this same day, sixty African-American ministers from ten southern states gathered in Atlanta for a meeting titled "Negro Leaders Conference on Non-Violent Integration." The next day the group renamed itself the Southern Christian Leadership Conference (SCLC), and King was selected as its president.

Other civil rights groups existed, but none met what King believed were the needs of that time. Two such groups, the National Urban League and the Congress of Racial Equality (CORE), were strong in northern states but had little impact in the South. The NAACP worked within the system to fight discrimination by filing lawsuits in federal courts. They won cases that removed barriers that made it difficult for African Americans to vote in the South.

But some of the NAACP's court victories were hollow ones, since the rulings were not enforced. King and the other members of the SCLC believed civil disobedience by average citizens, such as the bus boycott, would be more effective. To stress cooperation with the NAACP, King met with NAACP leaders soon after the formation of the SCLC. He said that while the NAACP continued its legal strategy, the SCLC would concentrate on "spiritual strategy."[1]

The SCLC had its work cut out for it. The bombings and shootings made it clear that some members of the white community in Montgomery were not going to accept bus segregation peacefully. Attitudes and prejudices die hard.

Yet much of white Montgomery was supportive. With the court decision now official, they were ready to accept it and go on with life. The daily newspaper, *The Montgomery Advertiser*, published an editorial condemning the bombings. Leading white citizens made public statements urging police to catch the persons responsible for the crimes.

The mayor of Montgomery decided that to stop the violence he would cancel all bus service. African-American Montgomery residents were once more without bus service. It appeared that a whole year's effort was wasted.

King held an emergency meeting at his church where he broke down and cried. He said out loud to those gathered, "Lord, I hope no one will have to die as a result of our struggle for freedom in Montgomery. Certainly, I don't want to die. But if anyone has to die, let it be me, Lord."[2]

The audience showed their love and support for King and responded by calling out "No! No!"[3] King was so overwhelmed with gratefulness he could not continue with his speech. Two aides had to help him from the podium.

But there was one more incident. On January 27, twelve sticks of dynamite were discovered on the porch of King's home. Luckily, they fizzled out before doing any damage. A few days later, several young white men were arrested in connection with the bombings. The arrests brought a sigh of relief among Montgomery's residents, even though no one was convicted of any crime. The violence ended, and the buses began rolling again.

King had just turned twenty-eight and was already known throughout the country as a commanding civil rights leader who had won a major victory. In February 1957, his picture was on the cover of *Time* magazine.

King was nervous, wondering what might next be expected from him.[4] He compared his leadership of the bus boycott to a magic act. He said, "I am really disturbed about how fast all this has happened to me. People will expect me to perform miracles for the rest of my life."[5]

At the time, most seemed to want speeches, not miracles. King was invited to talk before organizations across the country. He was also offered new jobs, but he turned them down. Dexter Avenue Baptist Church was his home.

One invitation took King to the country of Ghana in West Africa. Much of Africa at that time was under control of European countries. Ghana was one of the first to win its independence. King took time to visit the nation of Nigeria, too. He was shocked by its extreme poverty. King blamed it on the British colonial government and the fact that people in Nigeria were not allowed to govern themselves.

When he returned home, King compared colonial Africa to the United States. He said, "There is no basic difference between colonialism and racial segregation."[6] He said the cause of both was white supremacy.

The concept of white supremacy was still flourishing in the South. Segregationists there vowed to stop any more advancements for African Americans. Many whites thought blacks had already been given too much freedom. King might not have been able to provide any miracles, but he knew that the struggle for civil rights had just begun.

The federal government was moving very slowly toward any progress. President Dwight Eisenhower, elected in 1952, was a former general and a hero of World War II. He was a popular leader. However, Eisenhower spent thirty years in the military, which was at the time segregated. Segregation did not seem to bother Eisenhower as it might have bothered someone who grew up in an integrated society.

A weak Civil Rights Act was passed in 1957 during the Eisenhower administration. Although it was the first civil rights legislation passed in over eighty years, King and other civil rights leaders were unhappy with it. One part stated that anyone accused of violating one's voting rights would be given a trial in a state court. King wanted such cases tried in federal courts. It was unlikely that a jury in a southern state would rule in favor of an African American.

King asked to meet with Eisenhower to discuss this, but the President refused. So King thought of another way to draw attention to his concerns. One of his trusted advisors was a veteran civil rights leader named Bayard Rustin. The two of them, along with NAACP leader Roy Wilkins, led a prayer vigil at the steps of the Lincoln Memorial. The date was May 17, 1957. It was the third anniversary of the *Brown* v. *Board of Education* decision.

Over thirty thousand people were in the audience, including African-American celebrities such as baseball player Jackie Robinson (the first African American to play in the modern major leagues), actor Sidney Poitier, and singers Sammy Davis, Jr., and Harry Belafonte. King began speaking at 3 P.M. He called out:

Give us the ballot—and we will transform the salient misdeeds of bloodthirsty mobs into the abiding good deeds of orderly citizens. Give us the ballot—and we will fill our legislative halls with men of good will! . . . Give us the ballot—and we will quietly, lawfully implement the May 17, 1954 decision of the Supreme Court.[7]

Every time King repeated, "Give us the ballot," the crowd cheered with enthusiasm.

Eisenhower still would not meet with King or other African-American leaders, but he did take action in September 1957. The governor of Arkansas, Orval Faubus, refused to allow nine African-American students to enter a high school in Little Rock as a first step in racially integrating it. Eisenhower knew it was his duty to make sure the law was enforced. He sent the National Guard to protect the students. They were admitted, in spite of insults and screams from white mobs.

To King, the right to vote was the major key to equal rights and an end to segregation. The SCLC set a goal of registering millions of African-American voters . King spent the next two years flying from town to town, making speeches to raise money and change people's minds. This effort was called the Crusade for Citizenship.

During his travels, King also found time to write a book. In it he told the history of the Montgomery bus boycott. The book, *Stride Toward Freedom,* was published in 1958. In October 1957, something else was produced in the King household. The King's second child, Martin Luther King, III, was born.

Even with all of King's conscious efforts to gain sympathetic publicity for his cause, sometimes the best publicity comes about by accident. On September 3, 1958, King and his wife tried to enter a courthouse in Montgomery where his friend, Ralph Abernathy, had a case pending. A white guard refused to let the Kings inside. King asked to speak to Abernathy's lawyer, who was inside the building. To that request, the guard smiled and responded, "Boy, if you don't get the hell out of here, *you'll* need a lawyer."[8]

He was not even given a chance to leave. Another white guard said, "Boy, you've done it now—let's go."[9]

The two guards violently grabbed King and pushed him out of the courthouse and onto the street. Coretta cried as she tried to follow her husband. King begged her to stay put.

King was taken to jail and arrested on a false charge of loitering. He was manhandled by the white police officers. One slammed King against a jail wall. Another tried to ram his knee in King's groin.

A photographer who happened to be at the jail snapped a picture of a white officer twisting King's arm behind his back. The photo appeared in newspapers across the country, and King received more support and sympathy than he would have with any planned speech.

Two days later, King was found guilty and sentenced to pay a $10 fine plus $4 in court costs, or serve fourteen days in jail. He wanted to serve the jail term, but the Montgomery police chief did not want King to gain more sympathy. The chief paid the fine for King and let him go.

With that ordeal receiving national attention, King was asked to appear on NBC's *Today* show in New York City on September 20. Later that day, he was in a department store in Harlem, a predominantly African- American section of the city, signing his book for customers. King sat at a desk, while his fans waited patiently in line for an autograph.

A forty-two-year-old African-American woman pushed her way to the front of the line and approached King. She asked, "Are you Mr. King?" He responded, "Yes, I am." She swore at him and cried, "Luther King, I have been after you for five years."[10] She then pulled a long letter opener from her purse and stabbed King in the chest.

King was critically wounded and was hospitalized for ten days.

The attacker was Izola Ware Curry, a mentally unbalanced woman obsessed with King. She blamed him for everything wrong with her life. King said he felt no ill will towards Curry. While in the hospital, he said he hoped that "all thoughtful people will do all in their power to see that she gets the help she apparently needs."[11]

Curry was committed to a hospital for the criminally insane.

By the following February, King was well enough to travel. He and Coretta went to India where they met with Prime Minister Jawaharlal Nehru. The minister and the statesman discussed nonviolence and politics. In Bombay, King stayed in a house that once belonged to Mahatma Gandhi. He met with Gandhi's followers, who discussed their work with the Indian leader. King returned home with an even deeper commitment to nonviolence as a means of righting wrongs.

With King on the road more and more often, it was clear that he was unable to be both a full-time pastor and a national civil rights leader. In November 1959, he announced at a Sunday service that he was resigning his post at Dexter Avenue Baptist Church and moving back to Atlanta.

Daddy King welcomed his son home, where Martin joined his father as co-pastor of Ebenezer Baptist Church. There was some talk in Atlanta's African-American community that King was wealthy and no longer represented the people. King said, "The first thing some people ask me is, 'All right, Reverend, now where's the Cadillac?'"[12]

On the other hand, some conservative African Americans in Atlanta resented King's move to their city. They were "the old guard," established in their careers and comfortable in their financial situations. Their concern was that King might upset the status quo, which would drive a wedge between black and white Atlantans and hurt their standing.

In reality, King was not rich. He was basically unpaid by the SCLC and received $6,000 annually from the church. He drove not a Cadillac but a six-year-old Pontiac. In order to get along with "the old guard," King made sure the SCLC took no action in Atlanta. He used his Atlanta home only as a base for wider efforts.

King had hardly unpacked his suitcases when he heard of racial trouble in Greensboro, North Carolina. Restaurants were still segregated in Greensboro. On February 1, 1960, four black college students sat at a whites-only lunch counter in a department store.

They asked to be served and were refused. They sat for hours before leaving.

The next day the students were back. They promised they would keep sitting until they were served lunch. But the managers said the lunch counters were for whites only.

The students kept returning to the lunch counter on the following days. Their action was called a "sit-in."

Word of the sit-in spread rapidly, and soon they were joined at the lunch counter by both black and white students. Within forty days, sit-ins had spread to ten states. The students endured all kinds of taunting and harassment. White thugs poured ketchup, mustard, or salt on their heads, but the students just sat, quietly and nonviolently.

Out of the sit-ins, yet another civil rights group was formed, the Student Nonviolent Coordinating Committee (SNCC). Their goals were similar to those of the SCLC.

King and the SCLC had nothing to do with the sit-ins. They were started by students and spread in an unplanned manner. But King could be given credit for creating an atmosphere in which the sit-ins could take place. Several students said they remembered hearing about King and the Montgomery bus boycott while growing up.

In the middle of the sit-in action, King became headline news again. On February 17, he was arrested for not fully paying Alabama state income tax in 1956 and 1958. King was hurt by the charges.[13] He admitted he was not perfect but said that if he had "one virtue, it's honesty."[14]

A trial was held before an all-white male jury in late May. Arguments from both sides were heard, and King was found not guilty. The charges were false and were just an attempt by white authorities to destroy King. Martin showed no outward emotion when the verdict was read, but Coretta cried openly. She wrote, "It was a triumph of justice, a miracle that restored your faith in human good."[15]

The sit-ins continued through the summer of 1960. Students in Atlanta urged King to take part, but he had made the agreement that he would avoid any local protests.

There was another reason—politics. A presidential election was coming up. Vice President Richard Nixon of the Republican party was running against Senator John F. Kennedy of the Democratic party.

King had not formally endorsed either candidate. But he blasted Republicans in speeches, showing that his sympathies were with the Democrats. King was concerned that any involvement in civil rights unrest might reflect poorly on Kennedy.

The Atlanta students would not give up. They said King's participation would indicate his support for their cause. On October 19, King joined a sit-in at an Atlanta department store. He was arrested for trespassing. He could have paid $500 bond but elected to go to jail. His theory was that serving time for violating unjust laws would hopefully strike at America's conscience.

King shared a cell with other sit-in participants. One, Bernard Lee, said, "Our prize was that Martin Luther King—our leader—was there with us."[16]

After four days, the students were released. King was kept in jail, however. There was a complication in his case. After he had moved to Georgia earlier that year, King was required to get a Georgia driver's license in order to drive in that state. With his busy schedule, he had forgotten to do so. King was fined $25 and placed on a twelve-month probation.

With his arrest at the October sit-in, King was found guilty of violating the terms of his probation. He was sentenced to four months of hard labor in a Georgia public works camp. It was a very severe sentence for the crime.

King was transferred to a prison in Reidsville in rural Georgia and placed in a freezing cell crawling with cockroaches. The Democratic presidential candidate, John Kennedy, phoned Coretta and told her he would do all he could do to get King out of prison. Kennedy had his brother and campaign manager, Robert, call the judge who had ruled in King's case. He asked why King could not be released on bail. King was set free three days later. The event drew wide publicity across the country.

About a week later, the election was held. Kennedy was elected President.

Chapter 7

NO MORE WAITING

In spite of King's successes, not all African Americans admired him. Some with comfort- able lifestyles believed he was moving too quickly.

Others were more militant and thought King was moving too slowly. They resented his willingness to cooperate with white people, whom they saw as oppressors.

One vocal critic was a flamboyant black Muslim minister who had changed his name from Malcolm Little to Malcolm X. He said that his last name, Little, was a slave name, given to his ancestors by white slave owners. He urged his followers to also drop their slave names. The letter "X" represented his long forgotten ancestral name.

Malcolm X was a member of the Nation of Islam, an offshoot of the religion of Islam. The Nation of Islam was founded by an African American named Elijah Muhammad. Malcolm X preached in favor of black nationalism and against integration. He was also against nonviolence. He said African Americans should fight violence with violence.

In response to such urgings King said, "Nothing can be accomplished by violence. It only leads to new and complex social problems. I think it is unfortunate for the black nationalist movement. I think it is unfortunate for the health of our nation."[1]

Blacks who were submissive to whites were called "Uncle Toms" by militants, after a slave in the Harriet Beecher Stowe novel, *Uncle Tom's Cabin*. Because King stressed nonviolence and cooperation with whites, militants called him an "Uncle Tom."

This hurt King greatly.[2] In response to one critic, King defended himself by saying, "I don't want to talk about my personal suffering, but I've been in jail as much as anyone in the movement."[3]

In addition, there were disagreements among the various civil rights groups. It was not as if King was not an elected official. Voters had not chosen King as leader of the civil rights movement in the way that people elected a president. There were well-meaning African Americans who did not see King as their leader.

Many were in the NAACP. Its members did not like the protests used by King and the SCLC. To the NAACP, King was a young upstart getting the credit while the NAACP had been doing the work for decades.

Meanwhile, some SCLC people looked upon the NAACP in the same manner that militants viewed King. To them the NAACP was filled with "Uncle Toms" who placed too much faith in a racist legal system.

King hated the bickering and tried to play the role of peacemaker. He publicly supported the NAACP. In spite of the disagreements, the combined energy of the different groups did have positive results. In a decision called *Boynton* v. *Virginia* in 1960, the Supreme Court ruled that segregation in bus stations was illegal. (The court had ruled in 1946 in *Morgan* v. *Virginia* that segregation on interstate buses and trains was illegal but said nothing about bus stations.)

Despite the rulings, bus stations all over the South were still segregated. The civil rights group CORE decided in 1961 it would test those Supreme Court decisions. Under CORE's direction, blacks and white supporters boarded buses to travel through the heart of the South. They would try to enter "whites only" waiting rooms. These people were called "freedom riders."

Two buses of freedom riders left Washington, D.C., in early May 1961 with the final destination of New Orleans. There were a few minor incidents in Virginia, the Carolinas, and Georgia, but no major ones. In Atlanta, King had dinner with the freedom riders. Because he did not wish to draw publicity away from them, he stayed in Atlanta. The riders went on to Alabama where trouble was waiting.

In Anniston, about thirty miles across the Georgia border, an angry white mob set the first bus on fire. The passengers escaped, and there were no injuries.

Riders on the second bus were beaten by local whites, but the bus was able to continue west as far as Birmingham, about sixty miles away. As soon as the riders stepped off the bus there, they were beaten again, with baseball bats, lead pipes, and chains.

Most freedom riders could not take any more pain. They canceled the rest of the trip and flew to New Orleans. However, a small group was determined to continue the ride.

In Montgomery a mob of angry white men and women was waiting for them. The first person off the bus was a clean-cut white student named James Zwerg. Some white women yelled, "Kill the nigger-loving son of a bitch!"[4] A group of white men knocked Zwerg down and kicked out his front teeth.

As the white women encouraged the men to fight, people getting off the bus were kicked, punched, and beaten. This included reporters as well as freedom riders. Police arrived to break up the violence, but they were purposely late and arrested nobody.

In Washington, President Kennedy soon got word of the lawlessness. His brother, Robert Kennedy, now attorney general, sent six hundred federal marshals to Montgomery to keep the peace.

King saw the violence on television and flew in from Atlanta to lend support. He spoke that night in Abernathy's church in defense of the freedom riders. As he talked, a white mob of between three thousand and four thousand gathered in front of the church.[5] Before long they were throwing rocks and bottles into the church, breaking its stained glass windows.

Outside, federal marshals tried dispersing the mob with tear gas. Inside, people prayed and sang a song called, "We Shall Overcome," which had become the movement's anthem. After several hours, the crowd finally broke up.

A few days later, the freedom riders boarded buses in Montgomery under heavy guard. They rode to Jackson, Mississippi, and were arrested as soon as they tried to use the "whites only" facilities. They were sentenced to pay a $200 fine or spend two months in prison. They chose prison.

Freedom riders continued all summer long and accomplished what they set out to do. Segregation in bus terminals was soon truly outlawed, and segregation on interstate buses was no longer tolerated.

Some cities refused to follow the new law. One was Albany, Georgia. Nearly half of the fifty-six thousand citizens of Albany were African Americans. About 89 percent of them were poor.[6]

When African Americans tried entering "whites only" sections of the bus and train stations in Albany, they were arrested. King was encouraged by an Albany civil rights leader to come and energize the city's black residents.

King spoke on December 15, 1961, and the next day he led a march to city hall. He and the hundreds with him were arrested for parading without a permit. King was released on bail and went home to Atlanta.

In January 1962, Coretta gave birth to her and Martin's third child. He was a boy whom they named Dexter in honor of the Montgomery church where Martin first worked. A month later, King and Abernathy were back in Albany in court. They were found guilty of the parading charges and were told to stay out of Albany until their sentencing in July.

As in similar cases, King and Abernathy were sentenced to either pay a fine or spend time in jail. And as before, they chose to show the unfairness of the law by going to jail. But this time, something unusual happened.

After serving only one day of a forty-five day sentence, King and Abernathy were taken before Albany Police Chief Laurie Pritchett. The police chief told them their fines were paid.

King protested and said he had not authorized the fines to be paid. But Pritchett insisted that the fine was paid, and the two had to leave. Without being in jail, their message was diminished. King said to reporters, "This is one time I'm out of jail and I'm not happy to be out."[7]

The truth was that the fine was never paid. Albany's mayor, Asa Kelley, ordered King and Abernathy to be released. Kelley and Pritchett knew that keeping King in jail would bring more protesters to Albany. That was the last thing they wanted for their city.

King refused to accept this as the end of the Albany campaign. He urged SCLC members to ask for service at several of Albany's segregated public facilities and businesses. They did and were arrested. But Pritchett had studied King's method and knew how to ruin his protests.

Pritchett made sure there were no violent attacks on the protestors. He insisted that officers did not insult the protestors. When demonstrators prayed, Pritchett prayed along with them. The protest was going nowhere.

On July 24, there was chaos in the streets of Albany. A pregnant African-American woman was taking food to protestors in a prison outside the city. A deputy knocked her unconscious and kicked her in the stomach. The beating was so severe that she suffered a miscarriage.

That night, two thousand of Albany's African Americans reacted with anger to the beating. They demonstrated again. And when police tried making arrests, they fought back with bottles and stones. King's message of nonviolence was lost.

This caused a severe split in the movement. Leaders of SNCC felt nonviolence had taken them as far as it could. They thought more violence was the only answer. The NAACP was tired of attacks on African Americans. They felt a safer path of protest was through the courts. The Albany protest was falling apart.

King tried one more step to keep it alive. He and Abernathy led a small demonstration on July 27. They were arrested and sent to jail.

In early August, Coretta and the two older children visited Martin in jail. The children had by now become well acquainted with the legal segregation in the South. Little Yoki had earlier been denied entrance into a "whites only" Atlanta amusement park called Funtown.

They had never visited their father in jail before, though. King was taken out of his cell and into a hallway to meet his family. Yoki missed her father and said she wanted him to come home. She asked her mother why Daddy was in jail. Coretta answered so people may go where they please. Yoki smiled, "Good. Tell him to stay in jail until I can go to Funtown."[8] That brought a laugh from King.

Soon afterward, the city court suspended King and Abernathy's sentences. Again, they were released from jail.

The protest failed. Albany was still a segregated city.

One month later, the Ku Klux Klan dynamited four African-American churches in the Albany area. One SCLC member, Andrew Young, said King was so discouraged he thought of quitting the movement.[9] Yet Coretta appeared determined not to see Albany as a total failure. She wrote, "Though we had many problems with the Albany movement, it gave the people of Albany a new sense of dignity and respect, and an awareness of their plight that they did not have before."[10]

When Martin was home, it was a treat for his children. To them he was not a famous leader. He was just Daddy.

If Coretta left on church business or to run personal errands, Martin would baby-sit. He enjoyed roughhousing with the kids. Coretta would come home and often find the young ones piled on top of her husband. Sometimes Martin would put one of his children on top of the refrigerator and have him or her jump into his arms. Coretta was scared Martin might miss, but he never did. Quiet times were enjoyed, too. King spent evenings reading the children their favorite books.

His leisure moments at home were limited. If he was not involved with church work, he was out of town. But King was able to be home for the birth of his and Coretta's fourth and last child. It was a girl, Bernice, born on March 28, 1963.

Days later King was on his way to Birmingham, Alabama, one of the most segregated cities in the country. King and a minister named Fred Shuttlesworth knew it was time for a change. Shuttlesworth was leader of a civil rights group called the Alabama Christian Movement for Human Rights (ACMHR), which was similar to the SCLC in its methods and goals.

King was careful not to make Birmingham into another Albany. King's course of actions in Albany had not been well thought out, but he and Shuttlesworth carefully planned their campaign for Birmingham. It would begin with boycotts of segregated department stores and spread out from there.

There would likely not be the friction between different civil rights groups that took place in Albany. The NAACP was outlawed in Alabama, and the SNCC was not active there.

There was one potential problem in Birmingham, however. A new city government had been voted in. Some Birmingham residents sympathetic to King's cause thought the new government might make changes for the better. They thought King should wait and give the new city leaders a fair chance. A group of eight white Birmingham clergymen wrote a letter stating that King's actions were "unwise and untimely."[11] The letter was published in a Birmingham newspaper.

The letter disturbed King, who led a demonstration anyway. King was arrested and thrown into jail on April 12. In jail, he had time on his hands and began composing a response to the letter.

He had no blank sheets of paper and started by writing in the newspaper's margins. He continued on scraps of paper given to him by another inmate. He finished the response on a clean pad his lawyer had taken to him. By the time he was finished, King had written nine thousand words.

His response was written in the form of a letter. It was addressed to "MY DEAR FELLOW CLERGYMEN" and was dated April 16, 1963.[12] It has since become known as *Letter from Birmingham Jail* and is today regarded as one of the classic writings to emerge from the civil rights movement. His main point was that African Americans have waited long enough:

We have waited for more than 340 years for our constitutional and God-given rights. . . . Perhaps it is easy for those who have never felt the stinging darts of segregation to say, 'Wait.' But when you have seen vicious mobs lynch your mothers and fathers at will and drown your sisters and brothers at whim . . . when you suddenly find your tongue twisted and your speech stammering as you seek to explain to your six-year-old daughter why she can't go to the public amusement park that has just been advertised on television, and see tears welling up in her eyes when she is told that Funtown is closed to colored children . . . when you take a cross-country drive and find it necessary to sleep night after night in the uncomfortable corners of your automobile because no motel will accept you . . . when your first name becomes 'nigger' . . . then you will understand why we find it difficult to wait.[13]

Being in jail made it nearly impossible to continue his work with the antisegregation movement. After eight days in jail, King posted bail payment so he could be released.

Once on the outside, King noticed that the number of people protesting was small and appeared to have little effect. King and the SCLC leaders needed to add a spark to the campaign. Their solution was a controversial one.

Some children and high school students had asked to be part of the SCLC's protests. King knew the children could be injured or arrested, but if nothing changed in Birmingham, their lives would never get better. Maybe their participation would bring the needed change.

What would be called the Children's Crusade began on May 2, 1963, a hot, muggy Thursday. African-American children walked out of the Sixteenth Street Baptist Church in an almost endless stream and began marching through the streets. By the end of the day, about one thousand young people had been arrested.[14]

The next day even more children marched. Birmingham Police Chief Eugene (Bull) Connor, a well-known racist, demanded that the children return to the church.[15]

They kept on peacefully marching. Police stood by waiting for a command from Connor. Some carried sticks. Others held growling police dogs on leashes. Firefighters stood by with high-powered hoses, which carried seven hundred pounds of pressure and were able to strip the bark off a tree.[16]

Connor gave the command. The firemen turned on their hoses and powerful jets of water bowled over children as young as six. Some were smashed against buildings. Others literally had their clothes torn off by the force of the water. The police attacked adults and children alike with clubs. They let their police dogs loose. Some children were bitten. Most cried and ran. Bull Connor yelled, "I want to see the dogs work. Look at those niggers run."[17]

Pictures of the carnage appeared in newspapers and on television sets around the world. Most Americans were horrified by the sight of adults attacking children with clubs, dogs, and water hoses. President Kennedy said the event made him "sick" and admitted, "I can well understand why the Negroes of Birmingham are tired of being asked to be patient."[18]

Yet a march continued on an ever greater scale on Saturday. Connor kept the dogs locked up but allowed the firefighters to use their hoses to drive protesters away. In response, some African-American adults threw rocks at the police.

On Sunday, there was another march. Connor had his force ready. He called to the marchers to turn back. When they kept going, he screamed to his troops to turn on the hoses. But they did not. Connor's men held their hoses and dogs and refused to obey orders. They let the marchers proceed.

On Monday there was another march. But this time the fire hoses were used again.

The jails of Birmingham were by then filled. More protestors were arrested, but the police had no place to put them. King's ultimate goal of filling the jails worked. With public sentiment sorely against them and no more room for prisoners, the officials of Birmingham knew they were beaten. They met with King and SCLC leaders, and by Friday, an agreement had been reached. Birmingham's downtown stores were ordered to be fully segregated within ninety days.

Chapter 8

"I've Been to the Mountaintop"

The violence in Birmingham was not over yet. White racists were not going to accept integration without a fight. King's brother, A.D. King, lived in Birmingham, and his house was bombed. Fortunately, nobody was injured. The motel that King and the SCLC had used as their headquarters was also bombed. This time there were injuries.

Out of anger and in retaliation, African Americans in Birmingham took to the streets and rioted. King flew back to Birmingham to try to calm the people. President Kennedy rushed three thousand federal troops to the outskirts of the city to be used if needed. The bombings ceased, and on May 23, the Alabama Supreme Court officially voided all segregation laws.

It was in August that King gave his momentous address at the Lincoln Memorial in Washington. The militant minister, Malcolm X, did not approve. He referred to the march as the "Farce on Washington."[1] However, the event was very well received by the overwhelming majority of African Americans.

In public, King was a confident speaker who did not appear easily hurt. The public never could have known that privately he was sensitive and became depressed when hearing strong criticism.[2] Sometimes, the depression brought on attacks of hiccups that could last hours. But when he spoke before a group, he was able to control his emotions and mask his feelings of hurt and depression.

Less than three weeks after the cheers in Washington had settled down, there came proof that Birmingham was still home to hatred. A bomb exploded during a Sunday service in a church there that had been a rallying point for African Americans. Four girls— one age eleven and three ages fourteen—were killed.

Coretta wrote, "It was a devastating shock to Martin and me that anyone could have such hate in his heart as to kill innocent children."[3] Some African Americans urged others to arm themselves. But Christopher McNair, whose daughter Denise was among the victims, stated, "I'm not for that. What good would Denise have done with a machine gun in her hand?"[4]

Just two months later, on November 22, 1963, President Kennedy was assassinated in Dallas, Texas. When King heard the news, he said to Coretta, "That's the way I'm going to go. I told you this is a sick society."[5]

She said nothing in response.[6]

King's prominence made him an even greater concern for his enemies, which included powerful people. The most notable was J. Edgar Hoover, director of the Federal Bureau of Investigation (FBI). The FBI is the chief investigative branch of the United States Department of Justice.

For forty-eight years, from 1924 to 1972, Hoover was the FBI's director. He was a staunch anti-communist who harassed and watched closely those he suspected of being pro-communist. In the early 1960s, the Cold War was raging. "Cold War" is a term used to describe hostilities between the United States and the former Soviet Union, which had a communist system of government. Because no battles were actually fought, this period is referred to as the "Cold War."

The Cold War stemmed from the distrust each country had for one another. Basically, the Soviet Union did not trust the intentions of the United States, and many Americans believed the Soviets wished to conquer the United States. Because of this, many Americans feared communist influence. To be labeled a communist could be devastating to one's career and goals.

Hoover was no admirer of King. In a 1964 interview, he publicly called King "the world's greatest liar."[7] Privately, he called King "one of the lowest characters in the country."[8] Hoover ordered the telephones in King's home and office bugged so the FBI could listen to his private conversations. Under Hoover's direction, the FBI also sent King threatening anonymous letters.[9]

In truth, some of King's associates had past ties to or associations with members of the Communist party.[10] But most accusations were groundless. The SCLC had a firm policy against hiring communists, and King himself publicly stated his disagreement with the communist antireligion philosophy.

Hoover also tried to damage King by claiming that King was unfaithful to his wife. It is likely that King, away from his home and wife much of the time, was guilty of extramarital affairs.[11] An aide, Michael Harrington, said temptations were always present and that women of all races often made passes at King.[12]

King's behavior contradicted his teachings as a minister. In response, King felt tremendous pain and guilt as a result of his actions.[13]

The fact that King had dominated the news in 1963 was acknowledged at the end of the year. *Time* magazine selected Martin Luther King as their "Man of the Year." *Time* called King "the symbol of the (Negro) Revolution."[14]

Indeed, King was recognized earlier in 1963 as the leader of the civil rights movement by another major news magazine, *Newsweek*. In July, *Newsweek* reported results of a poll of African Americans ranking activists in the movement. *Newsweek* said, "In the Negro's eyes, one leader . . . towers above all others in the field. The leader is the Rev. Martin Luther King, Jr."[15]

It was King who was called when African Americans felt threatened. St. Augustine, Florida, is known today as the oldest permanent European community in the United States and a tourist destination. While it was a tourist destination in 1964, St. Augustine was also another segregated city of the deep South. What made it stand out was a reign of terror against black people there.

In one of the most shocking incidents, four African Americans were kidnapped by the Ku Klux Klan and beaten unconscious. The Klan members were planning to set the four men on fire. One asked, "Did you ever smell a nigger burn? It's a mighty sweet smell."[16] Those plans were stopped when a sheriff arrived at the last minute.

King wanted to expose the racism that existed in St. Augustine. On May 28, 1964, the SCLC led a march there. It came to an abrupt end when the marchers were attacked by thugs armed with bicycle chains and pipes. Violence against blacks continued in St. Augustine over the next two months.

To the delight of the SCLC, a white federal judge verbally blasted the city's racist leaders in July. The judge ordered a biracial group to begin talks to settle their differences. He further ruled that St. Augustine's motels and restaurants were to be integrated.

To demonstrate their good faith in the ruling, King and his staff went back home to Atlanta. But the ever-present KKK continued its bullying tactics. Regardless of the judge's decision, it would be some time before St. Augustine was fully integrated.

The new President, Lyndon Johnson, refused to take an official stand on the St. Augustine troubles, but there was some good news from Washington. The Civil Rights Act of 1964 was passed. King was present as Johnson signed it into law on July 2.

Laws cannot change attitudes, however, and later that month the Ku Klux Klan struck again, this time in the small town of Philadelphia, Mississippi. The KKK savagely murdered three volunteers—two Jewish white males and one African-American male—working for CORE. CORE and SNCC and volunteers of all races had been traveling through the South in 1964 urging African Americans to register to vote. The campaign was called "Freedom Summer."

After three years, nineteen men were put on trial for the murders. Included were the town's sheriff and his deputy. Authorities believed it would be impossible to get a murder conviction in a case like this in Mississippi in the mid-1960s. In hopes of getting some kind of conviction, the authorities charged the nineteen men not with murder but with violating the civil rights of the victims.

Seven of the nineteen were found guilty and sentenced to prison terms ranging from three to ten years. Even though the official charge was not murder, this was the first time in Mississippi that a jury found KKK members guilty of any charges involving a murder of African Americans or civil rights workers.[17]

Meanwhile, the patience of African Americans in the North was wearing thin. Out of frustration over their poor living conditions, African Americans rioted in Newark, New Jersey, the Harlem section of New York City, and Chicago. King went to Harlem at the request of New York's mayor, Robert Wagner. But he was booed by residents who saw him as an outsider interfering in their problems. He also overheard biting anti-Jewish comments among Harlem's residents.

King was hurt and troubled.[18] He told the people of Harlem that violence would make matters worse. In response to the anti-Semitism, King said, "I solemnly pledge to do my utmost to uphold the fair name of Jews. Not only because we need their friendship, and surely we do, but mainly because bigotry in any form is an affront to us all."[19]

As usual, he faced critics who once again said the movement was going too quickly. King argued that such charges "are both cruel and dangerous. The Negro is not going nearly fast enough, and claims to the contrary only play into the hands of those who believe that violence is the only means by which the Negro will get anywhere."[20]

King spent much of the rest of 1964 in the South on the SCLC's voting rights campaign called "People to People." At the year's end, he was honored with a special award, the Nobel Peace Prize for 1964. Nobel prizes pay tribute to people of any country who have made positive achievements for mankind. They are given in the sciences, the arts, and economics, but the most revered prize might be the one for peace.

Along with the award came over $54,000 in cash. King announced that he would donate "every penny" to civil rights causes.[21] He also said:

> I do not consider this merely an honor to me personally, but a tribute to the discipline, wise restraint, and majestic courage of the millions of gallant Negroes and white persons of good will who have followed a nonviolent course in seeking to establish a reign of justice and a rule of love across this nation of ours.[22]

King flew to Norway with the Abernathys to accept the prize. Soon he was back home, continuing the SCLC's voting rights campaign.

His next stop would be the small city of Selma, Alabama. Few people outside of the deep South in 1965 had heard of Selma. But since then, its very name evokes images of the madness of intolerance.

A voting rights campaign began in Selma in 1964, but it was not proceeding well. King and Abernathy helped out by leading marches in January 1965. In response, Selma Sheriff Jim Clark ordered mass arrests of the marchers. Peaceful demonstrations and arrests continued over the next few weeks.

After a nonviolent African American named Jimmie Lee Jackson was killed by Alabama state troopers in February, King and the SCLC decided to lead a march on foot from Selma to the state capital of Montgomery. It would be a fifty-mile-long hike, planned to take five days. In Montgomery they hoped to meet Governor George Wallace to have him address their grievances. Wallace was an admitted segregationist. At his inauguration, he promised, "Segregation now. Segregation tomorrow. Segregation forever."[23]

The march, scheduled to begin Sunday, March 7, was banned by the governor. But the protesters began walking anyway. They believed they would be arrested for marching without a permit and would draw attention to their concerns that way. But as soon as they crossed the Edmund Pettis Bridge to step outside Selma's city limits, they were beaten by Jim Clark and his men. White bystanders cheered Clark on.

One marcher was John Lewis, a founder of SNCC. Lewis remembered:

> We came to the apex of the bridge. You saw a sea of blue— Alabama state troopers. We kept walking, they started towards us, beating us with nightsticks, trampling us with horses, beating us with bull whips, using their tear gas.[24]

The day became known as "Bloody Sunday."

The next day, King called for members of the clergy of all religions to come to Selma in a show of support. Due to a federal judge's orders, King was able to lead only a shortened, symbolic march on March 9. But he asked those from out of town to stay for a real march to Montgomery twelve days later. Among them was James Reeb, a white Unitarian minister from Boston.

It turned out to be a fatal decision. Reeb and two other white ministers were beaten by a white mob. Reeb died from his wounds.

While the death of Jimmie Lee Jackson drew little reaction in the rest of the country, the death of white minister James Reeb from the North drew outrage. President Johnson went on national television on March 15 and introduced a voting rights bill.

The President ended his speech with the words of the civil rights anthem. He said, "It's not just Negroes but really it's all of us who must overcome the crippling legacy of bigotry and injustice. And we shall overcome."[25]

On March 21, King and Abernathy led over three thousand marchers across the Edmund Pettis Bridge to Montgomery. They reached Montgomery on March 24. At a rally at the state capital, King stressed the importance of the voting rights bill. He said, "The Civil Rights Act of 1964 gave Negroes some part of their rightful dignity, but without the right to vote it was dignity without strength."[26]

There was tragedy after that triumph, however. The next night, a white female civil rights worker named Viola Liuzzo was shot to death by three members of the Ku Klux Klan. The three were ultimately found guilty of violating Liuzzo's civil rights.

While the Selma campaign was going on in the South, there was some jarring news from the North. On February 21, 1965, Malcolm X was assassinated in Harlem. Three members of the Nation of Islam were convicted of the crime. Malcolm had split from Muhammad's antiwhite Muslim sect in 1964. He seemed to be changing his attitude toward one of acceptance of white people.

Though Malcolm X was dead, black militancy was growing. Some groups, especially the SNCC, drifted away from nonviolence. Under leaders such as Stokely Carmichael and H. Rap Brown, the SNCC advocated black nationalism and black militancy. The slogan used was "Black Power."

Brown said, "If America don't come around we (are) going (to) burn it down, brother . . . . We are going to burn it down if we don't get our share of it."[27]

White Americans were outraged and terrified. King was very disturbed. To him, "Black Power" meant black supremacy, which was as bad an idea as white supremacy.[28]

The next year King turned his attention to the North. In 1965 there had been a deadly race riot in the mostly African-American section of Los Angeles called Watts. King saw poverty and unemployment as two main reasons behind the riot. He thought Chicago would be the next city to explode if something was not done about the poverty and segregation there.

Some of King's aides thought going north was a mistake. King was better known and loved in the South. Also, there was no legal segregation in Chicago as there had been in the South. The city was segregated because of poverty, not the law.

The aides were right. In 1966 King led marches into white sections of Chicago to draw attention to the poor conditions in black sections. The marches stirred up the anger of white residents and appeared to do little good.

But they did succeed at showing that bigotry was not limited to the South. Television viewers watching the news saw marchers step past white people holding signs reading, "The only way to end niggers is to exterminate," and "The zoo wants you."[29]

In the summer of 1966, King's fears were realized. A riot broke out in Chicago. It seemed to some that King's message of nonviolence was losing its appeal.

In order to salvage some good out of his many months in Chicago, King turned his attention specifically to unemployment. The SCLC had success with an economic program in Atlanta called Operation Breadbasket. In this program, businesses that did not hire or promote African Americans were boycotted. King tried

Operation Breadbasket in Chicago and placed a young volunteer named Jesse Jackson in charge. It was an amazing success. In less than a year, it was responsible for twenty-two hundred jobs for African Americans in Chicago.

In January 1967, King first criticized the Vietnam War, which was raging. Within three months, he had become an outspoken opponent. In a speech on April 4, he cried out against the many who were dying in the war. King added that money that was going to fight the war would be better spent fighting poverty at home. In doing so, he angered many people, including members of the NAACP.

In order to make known his feelings about poverty, King believed a huge gathering in Washington along the lines of the 1963 March on Washington was needed. He began planning in the summer of 1967 what would be called the "Poor People's March." The march would take place in the summer of 1968.

After limited success in Chicago, King was looking for a campaign that would draw positive publicity for the SCLC. Militant organizations and leaders were dominating the headlines he once made.

In February 1968, sanitation workers went on strike in the city of Memphis, Tennessee. The overwhelming majority were African-American, and they were vastly underpaid in what was a thankless and grueling job.

King was asked by a Memphis minister named James Lawson to come help. King believed this might be the campaign to rebuild the SCLC's image. Memphis is located just across the Mississippi border in the deep South. King was not a stranger here as he was in Chicago.

King first flew to Memphis on March 18 and was warmly greeted by thousands of supporters. Over the next two weeks, he alternated trips to Memphis with other speaking engagements. On March 25, King spoke before the annual meeting of the Rabbinical Assembly in the Catskill Mountains of New York. The rabbis gave King a personal greeting by singing "We Shall Overcome" in Hebrew.

On March 28, King was back in Memphis to lead a march in support of the striking sanitation workers. But some militant young people, impatient with King's nonviolence, seized control of the event and rioted.

King flew back to Atlanta, then returned to Memphis on April 3. He planned to lead another march, a peaceful one, on April 5. Extra measures were taken to avoid violence.

The evening of April 3, King was resting in his room at the Lorraine Motel near downtown. That night, King sent Ralph Abernathy to speak in his place before a large crowd at a black church. King was weary and in need of rest. But the people there wanted to hear King. So King went and gave what was a prophetic speech. He referred to the attempt on his life in 1958 and talked about recent threats against his life. He ended with these words:

We've got some difficult days ahead. But it doesn't matter with me now. Because I've been to the mountaintop. And I don't mind. Like anybody, I would like to live a long life. Longevity has its place. But I'm not concerned about that now. I just want to do God's will. . . . I've seen the promised land. I may not get there with you. But I would like you to know tonight, that we, as a people will get to the promised land. And I'm happy tonight. I'm not worried about anything. I'm not fearing any man. Mine eyes have seen the glory of the coming of the Lord.[30]

The next evening, April 4, King stepped onto the motel balcony as he and some aides were about to leave for dinner at a friend's house. At about 6 P.M., a shot rang out. King was struck in the neck and jaw with a single bullet. Within an hour, he was pronounced dead.

Chapter 9

THE YEARS AFTER

Newspaper headlines the next morning blasted the news of Dr. King's assassination. World leaders reacted with stunned sadness. The prime minister of India, Indira Gandhi, said King's death "is a setback to mankind's search for the light."[1] The foreign minister of Israel, Abba Eban, said King was "an historic figure in the struggle for freedom and equality. His work will live long after him."[2]

At home, baseball player Jackie Robinson called the murder "the most disturbing and distressing thing we've had to face in a long time."[3] Roy Wilkins, executive director of the NAACP, said that King "was a man of peace, of dedication, of great courage. His senseless assassination solves nothing. It will not stay the civil rights movement, it will instead spur it to greater activity."[4]

President Lyndon Johnson postponed an official trip to Hawaii and went on national television. He announced, "We have been saddened," and ordered that flags on all federal buildings be lowered to half mast.[5] He then added, "I ask every American citizen to reject the blind violence that has struck Dr. King who lived by non-violence."[6]

But it was not to be. In cities across the nation, African Americans took their anger and frustration over King's violent death to the streets. There were 168 riots across the United States.[7] The worst hit was the nation's capital, Washington, D.C. Ten people died there, and arson fires could be seen from the windows of the White House, although the President was never in any serious danger.

In Memphis, a huge search got underway for King's assassin. The investigation soon stretched well beyond Memphis. All evidence pointed to a petty criminal and prison escapee named James Earl Ray. One of the biggest manhunts in history ended two months and four days after the shooting when Ray was arrested in London, England, on June 8. (Ironically, Ray's capture was announced on television during the funeral of King's old friend, Senator Robert Kennedy, who had been assassinated just days earlier.)

Ray was never tried. On March 10, 1969, he pleaded guilty to first degree murder in King's death and was sentenced to ninety-nine years in prison. However, while pleading guilty, Ray said he disagreed "with the theory that there was no conspiracy."[8]

Unfortunately, the presiding judge, J. Preston Battle, Jr., was legally unable to question Ray any further about his comment. Battle was legally unable to ask Ray to name names. Ray's guilty plea was legal only if he gave it "without threats, without pressure."[9] If the judge asked for names or other related facts, it could have been interpreted as "pressure," and Ray's guilty plea might have been overturned by the Supreme Court. Judge Battle could only continue with the required, standard legal procedure.[10]

Ray's guilty plea and the lack of a trial left many unanswered questions about King's assassination. In the years since the murder,

Ray has changed his story. He now says he was framed and did not shoot King. Many who believe Ray is guilty believe he shot King as part of a plot. Ray died in prison in Tennessee in 1998.

The King family was not through with tragedy. Martin's mother, Alberta King, was shot and killed while playing the organ in a church service in Atlanta on June 30, 1974. A church deacon was killed, too. The gunman was a deranged African American named Marcus Wayne Chenault who said he hated all Christians. He received a death sentence, which was later converted to life in prison, partly because the King family opposes the death penalty. Chenault died in prison of a stroke in August 1995.

Martin Luther King, Sr., (Daddy King) died of natural causes on November 11, 1984.

In 1983 President Ronald Reagan signed a bill making Dr. King's birthday a federal holiday. Martin Luther King, Jr., Day was first celebrated on January 15, 1986.

Coretta Scott King carried on her husband's message until her death on January 30, 2006. She was the founder of the Martin Luther King, Jr., Center for Non-Violent Social Change in Atlanta. Son Dexter King is the chairman of the King Center. Yolanda King was an actress until her death in 2007. Reverend Bernice King is a Baptist minister based in Atlanta, and Martin Luther King, III, is now a human rights advocate.

African Americans have made many advances in the years since King's death. In fact, it was in 1967, the year before King died, that African Americans were first elected as mayors of two major American cities. Carl Stokes became mayor of Cleveland, Ohio, and Richard Hatcher was voted mayor of Gary, Indiana.

There is nothing unusual about African Americans in such high civic positions today. The three biggest cities in the United States—New York, Chicago, and Los Angeles—have all elected African-American mayors. Even the citizens of Birmingham, Alabama, elected an African American, Richard Arrington, as their mayor.

In 1991 the two biggest heroes to emerge from the Persian Gulf War were General H. Norman Schwartzkopf, a white man, and General Colin Powell, a black man.

In 1992 Carol Moseley Braun of Illinois was elected to the United States Senate, becoming the first female African-American United States Senator.

John Lewis, SNCC founder, who was beaten during the violence in Selma in 1965, was elected to the United States House of Representatives from Georgia in 1986.

In March 1995, John Lewis, Coretta Scott King, Jesse Jackson, and other civil rights notables led about two thousand people in a march in Selma commemorating the original march thirty years earlier. Lewis and former King aide Hosea Williams were given the key to the city by Mayor Joe Smitherman. Smitherman was mayor when the first march took place. At that time, he was a strict supporter of segregation.

Smitherman admitted in 1995 he was wrong thirty years earlier. He said of the original marchers:

I thought they were outside agitators and if they would go away we could handle our own problems, which I know now we couldn't have. Looking back I realize that had I been black I would have been out there marching, too.[11]

In 1965 there were 250 African-American registered voters in Selma. In 1995 the total was 20,573 African-American registered voters. That has made a difference in this city that is 58 percent African American. There were no African-American elected officials in 1965. In March 1995, six of the eleven Selma school board members and five of the nine Selma city council members were African American.[12]

Perhaps another example of how much progress had been made in terms of tolerance may have been the 1990 election of L. Douglas Wilder as governor of Virginia. Wilder thereby became the first elected African-American governor in the nation. What was remarkable is that he was elected not only from a southern state but the very state that was home to the capital of the Confederacy.

Wilder explored running for President in 1992 but dropped out before the first primary election. However, it was in 1984 that former King advisor Jesse Jackson became the first African American to try to become the nominee of a major party. He lost the Democratic nomination to Walter Mondale. Jackson also ran for the Democratic nomination for President in 1988 but lost to Michael Dukakis. Nevertheless, 7 million Americans voted for Jackson in the primaries. Both Mondale and Dukakis lost their respective presidential elections to Republicans. In the fall of 1995, there was a large movement to draft Colin Powell as a candidate for President. After much consideration, Powell decided he was not ready to take on the job.

In 2008, Illinois senator Barack Obama, and African-American community activist from Chicago, won the nomination to be the Democrats' presidential candidate. In November 2008, he defeated

John McCain to become the 44th president of the United Sates. In 2012, Obama won reelection by a wide margin over Massachusetts governor Mitt Romney.

Governor George Wallace of Alabama was himself the victim of an assassination attempt in 1972. He was left partially paralyzed and in a wheelchair. Wallace admitted in 1974 he was wrong on segregation. He successfully courted African-American voters when he won elections for governor in 1974 and 1982.

In 1987, Reverend Jesse Jackson met with Wallace at the Wallace home in Alabama. Wallace asked Jackson, "Would you pray for me?"[13] They joined hands and prayed together. Wallace's son remembered:

At the end of the prayer there were tears in my eyes, tears in my father's eyes, and tears in Reverend Jackson's eyes. And my father looked at Reverend Jackson and said, "Jesse, I love you." Reverend Jackson looked at my father and said, "Governor, I love you."[14]

The civil rights movement was also a springboard for other movements. That includes those for the advancements of women, Hispanic Americans, Native Americans, and homosexuals.

But in spite of the continued striving for equality by oppressed groups, by the early 1980s the United States government had taken a more conservative turn. President Ronald Reagan's and George Bush's appointees to the United States Supreme Court were conservatives that replaced retiring liberal and moderate judges. Ironically, one of the most conservative new Justices is Clarence Thomas, an African American. The Court has since made several rulings striking down civil rights protections.

Although legal segregation and voting literacy tests are things of the past, there certainly is still racism in America. When African-

American baseball player Henry Aaron was approaching Babe Ruth's all-time home run record in 1975, many Americans could not handle the thought of a African-American man breaking a white man's record. Aaron received one hundred thousand pieces of hate mail, including threats on his life.[15]

In 1981, an African-American man was lynched in Alabama by the Ku Klux Klan. In 1988 a hate group called the White Aryan Resistance organized the killing of an Ethiopian man by skinheads in Portland, Oregon.[16] In 1991 David Duke, a former top level KKK member, received the Republican nomination for governor of Louisiana. Duke publicly renounced his KKK past and claimed to have moderated his once racist views. Many did not believe him. There was a massive effort to rally African Americans and other minorities to vote in Louisiana, and Duke was defeated in the general election.

The Ku Klux Klan and hundreds of other hate groups are active in the United States today. Hate crimes against African Americans, Hispanic Americans , Jews, Asian Americans, homosexuals, and other minorities are committed by neo-Nazi skinheads and other white supremacist groups with some regularity.

How can such disparities between African-American accomplishments and racial hatred be explained? Some analysts say the United States is still basically a racist country. Others say the United States is basically an open-minded country and that the hate crimes are a result of well organized but very small fringe groups.

But while there is still teeming African-American poverty and prejudice, there is a sizable African-American middle class that did not exist forty years ago. That kind of economic power is a direct result of King's marches for integration, voting rights, and respect. And although the names of King's African-American opponents like Stokely Carmichael and H. Rap Brown are mostly forgotten, Dr. King is celebrated as an American hero.

Perhaps Martin Luther King Jr.'s message is best summed up by former basketball star Kareem Abdul-Jabbar who remembered his youthful views of white people.

He recalled, "I had a more militant attitude and I wanted revenge. I wanted to hurt people. It was not until a long time later that I saw the wisdom of Dr. King's tactics."[17]

CHRONOLOGY

1929— Born in Atlanta, Georgia, on January 15.

1935— First brush with segregation when told he could no longer play with white friends.

1944— Enters Morehouse College at age fifteen; first taste of freedom as tobacco worker in Connecticut.

1947— Ordained a Baptist minister.

1948— Graduates from Morehouse College with B.A. in sociology; enters Crozer Theological Seminary in Chester, Pennsylvania.

1951— Graduates from Crozer as valedictorian; is admitted to Boston University School of Theology.

1953— Marries Coretta Scott on June 18.

1954— Accepts job at Dexter Avenue Baptist Church in Montgomery, Alabama.

1955— Daughter Yolanda (Yoki) is born; receives Ph.D. from Boston University.

1955–1956— Montgomery bus boycott.

1957— Forms Southern Christian Leadership Conference (SCLC); visits Africa; son Martin Luther, III, is born.

1958— Survives assassination attempt in Harlem.

1959— Visits India.

1960— Moves to Atlanta; becomes involved with sit-ins.

1961— Supports freedom riders in Montgomery.

1961-1962— Failed Albany, Georgia, campaign.

1962— Son Dexter is born.

1963— Daughter Bernice is born; plans Birmingham campaign and Children's Crusade; gives historic "I Have a Dream" speech at March on Washington; is named Time's "Man of the Year."

1964— Participates in St. Augustine, Florida, campaign; wins Nobel Peace Prize.

1965— Selma campaign with "Bloody Sunday" and march to Montgomery occur.

1966— Begins Operation Breadbasket in Chicago.

1967— First denounces Vietnam War; begins planning Poor People's March to Washington, D.C.

1968— Assassinated in Memphis on April 4; Poor People's March takes place under leadership of Ralph David Abernathy.

1986— Birthday of King first celebrated as federal holiday.

CHAPTER NOTES

Chapter 1. A Momentous Moment in Washington

1. "King," *Life,* Spring 1988, p. 29.

2. MPI Home Video, *Martin Luther King "I Have a Dream"* videotape, 1988.

3. Ibid.

4. Ibid.

Chapter 2. Separate but Unequal

1. William Robert Miller, *Martin Luther King, Jr.* (New York: Weybright and Talley, Inc., 1968), p. 7.

2. Lerone Bennett, Jr., *What Matter of Man: A Biography of Martin Luther King, Jr.* (Chicago: Johnson Publishing Company, Inc., 1968), p. 19.

3. Ibid.

4. Ibid., p. 20.

5. Personal interview with Dean Rowley, August 21, 1995.

6. Stephen B. Oates, *Let the Trumpet Sound: A Life of Martin Luther King, Jr.* (New York: HarperCollins Publishers, Inc., 1994), p. 14.

7. Ibid., p. 16.

8. Bennett, p. 25.

9. Ibid.

10. Oates, p. 17.

Chapter 3. The Collegiate Cleric

1. William Robert Miller, *Martin Luther King, Jr.* (New York: Weybright and Talley, Inc., 1968), p. 13.

2. Stephen B. Oates, *Let the Trumpet Sound: A Life of Martin Luther King, Jr.* (New York: HarperCollins Publishers, Inc., 1994), p. 19.

3. Ibid.

4. Ibid.

5. Lerone Bennett, Jr., *What Matter of Man: A Biography of Martin Luther King, Jr.* (Chicago: Johnson Publishing Company, Inc., 1968), p. 28.

6. Oates, p. 20.

7. Personal interview with Dean Rowley, August 21, 1995.

8. Miller, p. 16.

9. Edwin S. Gaustad, *A Documentary History of Religion in America Since 1865* (Grand Rapids, Mich.: William B. Eerdman's Publishing Co., 1990), pp. 120–121.

10. David J. Garrow, *Bearing The Cross: Martin Luther King, Jr. and the Southern Christian Leadership Conference* (New York: William Morrow and Company, 1986), p. 40.

Chapter 4. Marriage and a Major Move

1. Stephen B. Oates, *Let the Trumpet Sound: A Life of Martin Luther King, Jr.* (New York: HarperCollins Publishers, Inc., 1994), p. 36.

2. William Robert Miller, *Martin Luther King, Jr.* (New York: Weybright and Talley, Inc., 1968), p. 25.

3. Coretta Scott King, *My Life with Martin Luther King, Jr.* (New York: Puffin Books, 1993), p. 50.

4. Ibid., p. 52.

5. Ibid.

6. Ibid., p. 53.

7. Ibid., p. 54.

8. Ibid.

Chapter 5. Montgomery

1. Martin Luther King, "Alabama's Bus Boycott: What It's All About," *U.S. News and World Report,* August 3, 1956, p. 82.

2. Ellen Levine, *Freedom's Children* (New York: G.P. Putnam's Sons, 1993), pp. 24–25.

3. David J. Garrow, *Bearing the Cross: Martin Luther King, Jr. and the Southern Christian Leadership Conference* (New York: William Morrow and Company, Inc., 1986), p. 12.

4. Ibid.

5. Ibid.

6. *20-20* , television program, segment reported by Deborah Roberts, ABC News, August 18, 1995.

7. Ira Peck, *The Life and Words of Martin Luther King, Jr.* (New York: Scholastic, Inc., 1968), p. 25.

8. Coretta Scott King, *My Life with Martin Luther King, Jr.* (New York: Puffin Books, 1993), p. 105.

9. Ibid.

10. Garrow, p. 20.

11. Jim Bishop, *The Days of Martin Luther King, Jr.* (New York: G.P. Putnam's Sons, 1971), pp. 156–157.

12. Ibid., p. 155.

13. "King," *Life*, Spring, 1988, p. 29.

14. *The Class of the Twentieth Century* , television program, years 1963–1968, CEL Communications, Inc. and Arts and Entertainment Network, 1991.

15. Bishop, p. 165.

16. Ibid.

17. Ibid.

Chapter 6. Spiritual Strategy

1. Stephen B. Oates, *Let the Trumpet Sound: A Life of Martin Luther King, Jr.* (New York: HarperCollins Publishers, Inc., 1994), p. 124.

2. Jim Bishop, *The Days of Martin Luther King, Jr.* (New York: G.P. Putnam's Sons, 1971), p. 191.

3. Ibid.

4. Coretta Scott King, *My Life with Martin Luther King, Jr.* (New York: Puffin Books, 1993), p. 138.

5. Ibid.

6. David J. Garrow, *Bearing the Cross: Martin Luther King, Jr., and the Southern Christian Leadership Conference* (New York: William Morrow and Company, Inc., 1986), p. 91.

7. William Robert Miller, *Martin Luther King, Jr.* (New York: Weybright and Talley, Inc., 1968), p. 63.

8. Bishop, p. 208.

9. Ibid.

10. Lerone Bennett, Jr. *What Matter of Man: A Biography of Martin Luther King, Jr.* (Chicago: Johnson Publishing Company, Inc., 1968) , pp. 98–99.

11. Miller, p. 84.

12. Oates, p. 150.

13. Garrow, p. 129.

14. Ibid.

15. King, p. 171.

16. Oates, p. 162.

Chapter 7. No More Waiting

1. *The Class of the Twentieth Century* , television program, years 1963–1968, CEL Communications, Inc. and Arts and Entertainment Network, 1991.

2. Stephen B. Oates, *Let the Trumpet Sound: A Life of Martin Luther King, Jr.* (New York: HarperCollins Publishers, Inc., 1994), p. 130.

3. Lerone Bennett, Jr., *What Matter of Man: A Biography of Martin Luther King, Jr.* (Chicago: Johnson Publishing Company, Inc., 1968), p. 128.

4. Jim Bishop, *The Days of Martin Luther King, Jr.* (New York: G.P. Putnam's Sons, 1971), p. 252.

5. Ibid. p. 254.

6. William Robert Miller, *Martin Luther King, Jr.* (New York: Weybright and Talley, Inc., 1968), p. 113.

7. David J. Garrow, *Bearing the Cross: Martin Luther King, Jr. and the Southern Christian Leadership Conference* (New York: William Morrow and Company, Inc., 1986), p. 203.

8. "Visit with Martin Luther King," *Look*, February 12, 1963, p. 92.

9. Oates, p. 205.

10. Coretta Scott King, *My Life with Martin Luther King, Jr.* (New York: Puffin Books, 1993), p. 191.

11. Martin Luther King, Jr., *Why We Can't Wait* (New York: Mentor Books, 1964), p. 76.

12. Ibid.

13. Ibid., pp. 81–82.

14. Bennett, p. 152.

15. James Haskins, *The March on Washington* (New York: HarperCollins Publishers, Inc., 1993), p. 21.

16. Ely Landau, producer, *King: A Filmed Record: Montgomery to Memphis,* Pacific Arts Video, videotape, 1970, 1988.

17. Ibid.

18. Oates, p. 235.

Chapter 8. "I've Been to the Mountaintop"

1. James Haskins, *The March on Washington* (New York: HarperCollins Publishers, Inc., 1993), pp. 71–73.

2. Stephen B. Oates, *Let the Trumpet Sound: A Life of Martin Luther King, Jr.* (New York: HarperCollins Publishers, Inc., 1994), p. 281.

3. Coretta Scott King, *My Life with Martin Luther King, Jr.* (New York: Puffin Books, 1993), p. 225.

4. William Robert Miller, *Martin Luther King, Jr.* (New York: Weybright and Talley, Inc., 1968), p. 151.

5. Jim Bishop, *The Days of Martin Luther King, Jr.* (New York: G.P. Putnam's Sons, 1971), p. 336.

6. Ibid.

7. Martin L. Waldman and Linda Waldman, executive producers, *Biography: J. Edgar Hoover,* CEL Communications, Inc., and Arts and Entertainment Network, 1993.

8. David J. Garrow, *Bearing the Cross: Martin Luther King, Jr. and the Southern Christian Leadership Conference* (New York: William Morrow and Company, Inc., 1986), p. 360.

9. Waldman and Waldman.

10. Garrow, pp. 195, 200–201.

11. Ibid., p. 375.

12. Ibid.

13. Ibid., p. 376.

14. "Man Of The Year," *Time,* January 3, 1964, p. 13.

15. "The Big Man Is Martin Luther King, Jr.," *Newsweek,* July 29, 1963, p. 30.

16. Oates, p. 293.

17. Sara Bullard, executive editor, *Free At Last: A History of the Civil Rights Movement and Those Who Died in the Struggle* (Montgomery, Ala.: Southern Poverty Law Center, 1989), p. 68.

18. Oates, p. 306.

19. Ibid.

20. Martin Luther King, Jr., "Negroes Are Not Moving Too Fast," *Saturday Evening Post,* November, 1964, p. 8.

21. "Nobleman King," *Newsweek,* October 26, 1964, p. 77.

22. Ibid.

23. Bob Roy, executive producer, *Biography: George Wallace,* ABC News and Arts and Entertainment Network, 1994.

24. Ibid.

25. *The Class of The Twentieth Century* , television program, years 1963–1968, CEL Communications, Inc. and Arts and Entertainment Network, 1991.

26. Bullard, p. 31.

27. Patricia and Fredrick McKissack, *The Civil Rights Movement in America from 1865 to the Present* (Chicago: Children's Press, 1991), p. 257.

28. Bishop, p. 435.

29. Ely Landau, producer, *King, A Filmed Record: Montgomery to Memphis,* Pacific Arts Video, videotape, 1970, 1988.

30. Clayborne Carson, et. al., eds., *The Eyes on the Prize: Civil Rights Reader, Documents, Speeches, and Firsthand Accounts From The Black Freedom Struggle, 1954–1990* (New York: Penguin Books, 1991 and Blackside, Inc., 1991), pp. 418–419.

Chapter 9. The Years After

1. Associated Press, "King's Death Stuns World," *The Hartford Times,* April 5, 1968, p. 7A.

2. Ibid.

3. "A Turning Point: Toward Chaos or Rededication?" *The Hartford Times,* April 3, 1968, p. 17A.

4. Ibid.

5. Associated Press, "Johnson Saddened, Delays Hawaii Trip," *The Hartford Courant,* April 5, 1968, p. 1.

6. Ibid.

7. Patricia and Fredrick McKissack, *The Civil Rights Movement in America from 1865 to the Present* (Chicago: Children's Press, 1991), p. 260.

8. Associated Press, "Ray Enters Guilty Plea, Sentenced to 99 Years," *The Hartford Courant,* March 11, 1969, p. 1.

9. Gerald Frank, *An American Death* (New York: Bantam Books, 1972), p. 455.

10. Ibid.

11. Tom Watson, "A Returning Point for Rights Activists," *USA Today,* March 6, 1995, p. 3A.

12. "Selma, Ala., 30 years later" chart, *USA Today,* March 6, 1995, p. 3A.

13. Bob Roy, executive producer, *Biography: George Wallace,* ABC News and Arts and Entertainment Network, 1994.

14. Ibid.

15. Myron B. Pitts with Laurie Werner, "5 Questions," *USA Weekend,* April 7–9, 1995, p. 10.

16. Personal interview with Joe Roy, director of the Southern Poverty Law Center, Montgomery, Alabama, January 18, 1996. Based on case number A8911-07007, original case verdict rendered October 25, 1990, circuit court, state of Oregon.

17. *The Class of the Twentieth Century* , television program, years 1963–1968, CEL Communications, Inc. and Arts and Entertainment Network, 1991.

FURTHER READING

Duncan, Alice Faye. *The National Civil Rights Museum Celebrates Everyday People.* Mahwah, N.J.: BridgeWater Books, 1995.

Fireside, Harvey, and Sarah Betsy Fuller. *Brown v. Board of Education: Equal Schooling for All.* Springfield, N.J.: Enslow Publishers, 1994.

Haskins, James. *The Day Martin Luther King, Jr., Was Shot—A Photo History of the Civil Rights Movement.* New York: Scholastic, 1992.

———. *The March on Washington.* New York: HarperCollins Publishers, Inc., 1993.

King, Coretta Scott. *My Life With Martin Luther King, Jr.* Revised edition. New York: Puffin Books, 1993.

——— . *The Words of Martin Luther King, Jr.* New York: Newmarket Press, 1983.

King, Martin Luther, Jr. *Stride Toward Freedom: The Montgomery Story.* New York: Harper Brothers, 1958.

——— . *Why We Can't Wait.* New York: Harper & Row, 1964.

——— . *Where Do We Go From Here: Chaos or Community?* New York: Harper & Row, 1967.

Levine, Ellen. *Freedom's Children: Young Civil Rights Activists Tell Their Own Stories.* New York: G.P. Putnam's Sons, 1993.

McKissack, Patricia and Fredrick. *The Civil Rights Movement in America From 1865 to the Present.* Chicago: Children's Press, 1991.

O'Neill, Laurie A. *The Desegregation of Central High.* Brookfield, Conn.: Millbrook Press, 1994.

Stein, R. Conrad. *The Story of the Montgomery Bus Boycott.* Chicago: Children's Press, 1986.

INDEX